Kate!
Thank you so much for
help with everything. y...

I'M STILL HERE

From Heart Failure to Heart of a Champion

Johnnie Davis

ISBN: 0692872337
ISBN 13: 9780692872338
Library of Congress Control Number: 2017905565
Johnnie Davis, Charlotte, NC

DEDICATION

I want to dedicate this book to my beautiful wifesaver, Rachel Davis; my mother, Pauline Davis; Fire & Rescue team at Station 38 (Ret.) Captain Dale Cuff, (Ret.) Bill Petrea; Thomas Wright and Mark Bosemiller, and my neighbor Gary Sturgis. You all played a pivotal role in my being alive today and I love you with all my heart for it. I cannot thank you enough.`

FOREWORD

I've had the pleasure and opportunity to coach, train, lead, and support thousands of people from all over the world. I have been impacted by many life stories. Most of them will not get an opportunity to be told in public, change lives, shift perspectives, and inspire. This one does!

I met Johnnie back in 2015 and I was instantly impacted by his powerful story. The significant emotional event he went through became a beginning of something new, new intention, new meaning, and an opportunity to impact lives.

His message is clear, personal, and powerful. It represents the beauty of life and offers people from any level of success the opportunity to be more purposeful and grow. It shares clear principles and practical life strategies to not only appreciate the time we have, but also, to have more success in every area of life. Johnnie serves as an example of possibility, a model for transformation, and a grateful soldier of truth. Enjoy and grow.

—Rod Hairston, author of *Are You Up for The Challenge*

CHAPTER 1

JOHNNIE
MY DATE WITH DESTINY

"Good morning, Mr. Davis. My name is Dr. Peters and I will be your main doctor while you are here with us. How are you feeling today?"

I stared at Dr. Peters in disbelief. I couldn't believe that at thirty-four years old, I'd be lying in a hospital bed, hooked up to a bunch of machines. I've been an athlete for most of my life. Never smoked. Never drank more than an occasional beer.

"I've definitely had better days, doc, that's for sure," I responded. "I feel absolutely horrible. What's wrong with me?"

"I bet you do. I don't know how to tell you this, so I'm just going to tell it to you straight," he said, looking me in the eyes. I had to brace myself because it sounded very serious and I was preparing to hear the worst. In his strong accent, he continued. "Your heart is really, really bad. You have what's known as Congestive Heart Failure," and before he could finish his sentence, I stopped him.

"I have what? Heart failure? How?" He then went on to say that my heart was functioning at less than 10% and that right now I qualified for a heart transplant. "Wait a minute, doc. What do you mean I need a heart transplant? How did this happen to me?"

I was mortified! I looked over at the students standing around me, eager to hear the doctor's words, and yet all I wanted to do was run away. He rattled off a list of things that could possibly cause heart failure like obesity, drug use, diabetes, smoking, heart attack, etc. As I struggled to prop myself up, I looked at him and said, "Doc, I was just in Destin, Florida a few months ago, playing football on the beach! As you can see, I'm not overweight. In fact, I've always been an athlete and I've always worked out in the gym. I don't have diabetes, I'm not a smoker nor have I ever used any illegal drugs in my life, so I'm really confused as to what could be the cause of this!" He asked me if I had a cold or flu recently. I told him no. He then asked if I had a family history of heart issues and I told him not that I was aware of. My father had died from a heart ailment but he was a smoker and a drinker for most of his life. I didn't know of anyone on my mother's side of the family either that may have had a heart issue.

He said there were exceptions sometimes and that these things can just happen out of the blue. "We don't believe your condition is genetic because your artery walls are not thickened. That would indicate Hypertrophic Cardiomyopathy, which is more genetic in root cause. Your official diagnosis is Idiopathic Cardiomyopathy, which is a fancy way of saying that there is no known cause for your heart failure." He then said something that was really hard to swallow. Mr. Davis, had you waited just twenty-four hours to come to the hospital, I'm afraid you would have expired."

I immediately got choked up and had no words at that point. I looked at him in complete bewilderment. I could not believe what I was hearing. I zoned out completely. I saw his lips moving but I didn't hear anything that was coming out of his mouth. My mind just shut down because it was on information overload, I guess.

The more he spoke, the more I looked at him and, eventually, I snapped out of my trance. "Doc! Am I going to die?" I blurted out.

"Not today," he responded. "Because you are so young, you can make a full recovery." As he was speaking, the students were taking notes and looking at me as if I were an alien or something. It was bad enough that I was going through something like this, even worse to be watched by strangers while doing so. I asked the doctor if he could ask the group to step outside of my room. They made me feel uncomfortable. He obliged and told them to leave the room and wait outside.

He then stepped closer to me, put his stethoscope on my chest, and began to listen to my heartbeat. He took two fingers and started thumping on my chest to determine if my heart had enlarged. "Mr. Davis, your heart is the size of two hearts, so we have to somehow shrink it down. It may never go back to normal size but we definitely need it significantly smaller than it is now."

"Well, what's the next step?" I asked him. I didn't like the idea of having a heart transplant. I was still in a fog because I just could not wrap my head around what I was hearing.

"We can give you this experimental treatment of medication and see what happens. We've seen patients in your condition have favorable outcomes with these medications. However, I don't want to make any guarantees. We have to closely monitor you over the course of several months to see how your heart and body responds to the medication. If you are heading in the right direction with improved heart function, we will keep you on a regimen of prescription drugs. However, if there is no significant improvement over time, we may have to revisit the idea of a heart transplant. Otherwise, you may certainly die due to your heart giving out. Do you understand what I just said?"

I told him yes, clearly, though I needed a second to let it digest. I thought to myself, shit, man, what the hell is going on? This had to be some cruel joke or something. I must be living in a really bad dream. After a moment, I finally responded. "Well, let's go with the medications because the idea of you guys taking my heart out of my chest and replacing it with a different one sounds like a little bit more than I can even imagine right now."

He then asked me the million-dollar question that I knew would eventually come up. "Mr. Davis, why did you wait so long to seek medical attention? Surely you must have been experiencing serious symptoms, yes?"

I thought for a moment, then replied. "Doc, you have no idea."

"I'm interested in hearing your story," he said. "You are quite the buzz on this floor."

"Really, me?" I was surprised. "Why? I'm no celebrity or anything."

"I know, but, you see, you are the youngest person in the cardiac ward and just happen to be the healthiest sick person we've seen in years! You're going to have several doctors drop in on you to see how you're doing and ask you some questions. We've tested your blood for everything under the sun and still cannot determine why you are so sick. Your case is highly unusual, so everyone wants to come in and see you."

Are you freaking kidding me?

I laid there for a minute, staring at the ceiling, hoping some answers would just fall out of the sky. But, of course, none did. He pulled up a chair and began to listen to me talk. "Doc, don't you have to see more patients?"

"I have a few minutes to listen to your story," he said.

"What about your students? They are out in the hallway waiting for you."

He replied with a little smirk on his face. "Let them wait. They are not going anywhere. They will be here all day anyway."

With tears in my eyes, I said okay and told him I would give him the cliff's notes version as best I could.

"No worries, take your time. You're going to be here for a while yourself."

I said myself, this guy is a smart ass, but I like him. I'd never been so afraid in all my life.

CHAPTER 2
HOW IT ALL BEGAN

I t was late November, just after Thanksgiving, and I arrived in Destin, Florida. I was attending an Executive Retreat for all of the top sales leaders in our company at the time, and I was looking forward to the festivities. I was working as an Executive for a company that provided legal aid benefits to customers. I had never been to Destin but I heard it was a fantastic place to visit, especially during the fall season. When I left Charlotte, the cold was starting to set in, but the weather in Florida was like summer time, so it was game on!

While we were there, we partook in a myriad of activities like playing football on the beach, deep sea fishing in the gulf, and partying. Basically, having the best time ever. We were there for a week, but the most memorable part of the trip for me was the last day. We went deep sea fishing in the gulf and caught a tremendous amount of grouper. We decided to take the fish to a local restaurant and have them prepare it for us so that we could eat it later on that night at the party send-off.

Later that evening, we arrived at the restaurant and they did a phenomenal job with the food preparation and the fish was amazing. They filleted it, fried, grilled, baked, blackened, and sautéed it. Any way you could prepare fish, they did it for us and it was all so delicious. I ate so much, I felt like my stomach was going to burst. All of sudden, I began feeling a sharp pain in my stomach like I had bad indigestion. I sipped some ginger ale because that always helped to relieve an upset stomach. I sat there in my chair for a while and thought to myself, *Johnnie, you did it again. You went overboard on the fish, dude.* I couldn't just eat a few pieces like a normal person, I had to be greedy. I decided to take a walk to see if that helped. As I walked, I realized I had an insane amount of gas. The relief of letting it out on the walk was indescribable—even better than sex!

Later that night, we went back to our rooms and I noticed the same feeling I had at the restaurant. I thought it was gas again. Only this time, nothing was coming out. I was in writhing pain the whole night and didn't get a good night's sleep at all. I woke up the next day and the pain was still there, but now it was creeping up into my chest. I kept thinking it might have been bad indigestion, so I really didn't think too much of it. I caught the shuttle back to the airport and my stomach was throbbing in pain. I didn't know if I was going to be able to make it all the way back to Charlotte. Although it was a short direct flight, I had a long layover in Tennessee.

While in Tennessee, my chest began hurting to the point that it became difficult to breathe. I never in my life experienced anything like this before and I was getting concerned that something could really be wrong. I then quickly dismissed that thought and toughed it out all the way back to Charlotte.

The short plane ride from Tennessee seemed like an eternity. I couldn't wait to land, get off the plane, grab my bag, and get to my car. The first place I stopped was the pharmacy. I wanted to grab some over-the-counter indigestion medication and take it immediately. I thought that would knock whatever this was in my stomach and chest out. It seemed to the do the trick because I took the Mylanta as soon as I got back in the car to go home. No sooner than I opened the door to go in the house, the gas man came and it was major relief. I heard the angels in heaven singing *Hallelujah, Hallelujah*. But, alas, it was only temporary because shortly before nightfall that gnawing feeling of bad indigestion returned, and this time, I knew it wasn't gas.

I had no idea what it was but it was starting to really get to me. I began feeling weak and it was getting more difficult to catch my breath. The thought did come to mind that I should go and get this checked out, but I quickly talked myself out of it because I was too afraid to go the doctor. As stupid and as crazy as it sounds, I did what most guys do in this situation, nothing. However, I went online to WebMD and tried to self-diagnose. That didn't work out too well, either. Two weeks went by and my health was steadily declining. Instead of going to the doctor to get checked out, I went back to New Jersey to spend the Christmas holiday and New Year with my family. I relocated from New Jersey to Charlotte in March earlier that year and I had no family in North Carolina. So, I was excited to go home and be amongst familiar faces.

By this time, I noticed that I was considerably weak and just the mere thought of lugging my bag through the airport on Christmas day of all days scared the crap out of me. This was the absolute worst day to travel because the airport was a mob scene. I struggled through airport security, lugging my bag with the strength of ninety-year-old man and had to stop every so often to catch my breath. I thought I was going to collapse and die in the waiting area as I waited to board the plane. I was scared out of mind at that point because surely something was wrong with me but I was still in denial. Somewhere in the dark crevices of my mind, I was hoping this would all just go away.

I arrived in Newark Airport and peeled myself off the plane to get my bag from baggage claim. I picked up my bag then went outside to catch a cab. The driver looked at me and said, "Hey, buddy, are you okay? You don't look so good."

"I don't feel very well," I said to him, "but I will make it." I gave him the address to my mom's house and he took me there. When we arrived, he noticed that I was struggling to get out of the car, so he kindly took my bag out of the trunk for me. I put the bag over my shoulder and walked to my mom's front door and rang the bell.

My mom opened the door and her big smile turned into a look of concern immediately. She gave me a hug and I dropped the bag on the floor and greeted everyone in the house on my way to the kitchen. I was so tired, I just wanted to rest. Though the food smelled delicious, I had no appetite at all. The chest pain, shortness of breath, and fatigue had taken a toll on me and it robbed me of my appetite.

Later that night, I pulled my mom to the side away from everyone and told her how terrible I had been feeling. She looked at me and asked if I had eaten anything that day. I told I hadn't because I had no appetite. Besides, I had this feeling of bad indigestion and I didn't think that food would make that any better. She suggested I try eating something and I did, of course.

About an hour or so later, I vomited everything I had in me. I knew something was seriously wrong then because I never, and I mean never, vomited after eating my mother's food. After that episode, I said to myself, damn, bro, this is only day one of seven, what are you going to do for the rest of the week?

I told my mom what happened and she told me not to worry. She said she knew exactly what to give me that would help regain my strength and get rid of the indigestion. She gave me one of her all-natural home remedies which consisted of this nasty-tasting Aloe Vera gel. It was, by far, the worst thing I had ever tasted in my thirty-three years of living. Later on that night, I vomited that up, too. The next several days consisted of me vomiting all solid foods, so I tried eating soup instead. That seemed to be the only thing I could keep down though it wasn't very filling. Despite being happy to see my family, I had a miserable time because I felt terrible. I couldn't wait to get back home to Charlotte because I had made up my mind that I was going to go to the doctor.

January 6, 2006, my birthday arrived and it was time to go back home to Charlotte. I was excited because I turned thirty-four but I was nervous because I was still feeling absolutely horrible and I had no idea what was wrong with me. The thought of lugging my heavy bags through the airport once again was daunting to say the least. It was a necessary evil that had to be done because there was no one else there to do it.

I caught a cab to Newark Airport and once again struggled to get the bags out of the trunk of the car. It was a pathetic sight to see and the thought of it makes my eyes water. In the back of my mind, I thought I was going to die prematurely. I had all kinds of negative thoughts; I was scared to death. All I could do was pray to God and ask for guidance and direction because I had no idea what to do. I pulled those bags through the airport and up to the counter with all my might and I was sweating profusely.

The ticket agent asked, "Sir, are you okay? You don't look well."

"Thanks for asking; that was really nice of you. I'm okay," I said, though I wasn't feeling 100%. I checked my bags and went through security.

I boarded the airplane feeling miserable, but this time, I fell asleep immediately after sitting down. I didn't want to talk to any-one. I didn't want anything to drink or snack on, either; I just wanted to sleep. I shut my eyes, and in what felt like ten minutes later, I was back in Charlotte ready to deplane. I could not believe how much warmer it was in Charlotte versus New Jersey.

I walked over to baggage claim though I was thinking I could really use a ride on that buggy they use to cart seniors around or people with walking disabilities. I didn't care how I may have looked on that buggy, I was so tired and short of breath that I surely would have hopped on one if it came zooming by.

I began sweating again as I made my way over to baggage claim. I retrieved my bags and caught a ride with a friend who picked me up from the airport. I felt so sick on the way home, I was eager to get there and sleep in my bed. When I finally arrived at home, I left the luggage in the car, opened my door, and went straight to the sofa and slept for the remainder of the day. I had arrived in Charlotte from Newark at approximately 2:30 that afternoon. I didn't wake up until later on that night, past 10:00 p.m. Happy 34th birthday, Johnnie Davis. I should have been up partying and having a great time, but on the contrary, I was at home feeling like I was fighting to stay alive. Little did I know, that was actually true.

January 7th arrived, and by the grace of God, I woke up early that morning. I was not feeling well at all and I finally came to the realization that I had to go to the doctor to find out what was wrong with me. I ate a small breakfast, got dressed, and went to an urgent care facility in South Carolina. I filled out all the necessary paperwork and sat in the waiting room. I did not have medical insurance at the time nor did I have a regular primary physician, hence the reason I went to an urgent care facility.

My name was called and my heart sank to the pit of my stomach because I knew that something was wrong. I walked to the back of the office and met with the doctor. He was young, perhaps the same age I was or younger even. I remember saying to myself, *I hope he knows what he's doing!* I explained to him that my symptoms were shortness of breath, chest pain, weakness, extreme fatigue, and vomiting. Based on my description of the symptoms, he determined that I was experiencing a peptic ulcer. "Doc, an ulcer?" I asked. "I've never had stomach problems like that in my life, ever. How did you come up with that diagnosis?"

He began to explain that everyone has bacteria in their stomachs that lay dormant for most people, however, sometimes it could become active, which is called H Pylori. The more he explained, the more it just didn't add up. I knew something wasn't right about what he said but he was the doctor with a medical degree. He prescribed a regimen of antibiotics for me to take for fourteen days to kill the bacteria in my stomach and assured me that everything would go back to normal.

I was so relieved to hear that it was an ulcer, although I didn't agree with his diagnosis. But that was better than hearing, "Mr. Davis, you are going to die and there's nothing we can do to save you."

I went to the pharmacy to pick up the medication and it was expensive. With no insurance or prescription coverage, the total was over $400.00. I didn't care about the cost at that point, I just wanted relief from the pain and to go back to feeling like my normal self again. I brought the medication home and began taking it.

There were four different pills to take and I can still remember both the smell and taste of those nasty pills. I was advised to take the medication in its entirety for fourteen days but I was only able to take them for ten days because I had an allergic reaction to one of the pills which caused my heart to race. I read the fact sheets that came with the prescriptions and one of the side effects was rapid heartrate. My heart was racing so fast that I could see it beating through my shirt.

I called my mother and told her that I was having a heart attack and began crying on the phone like a baby. I was so scared, I had no clue what to do. I froze, I literally froze, and the grown man became that little boy who needed his mother.

"Johnnie, stop taking that medication," my mom said to me. "Don't take any more of it!" And I did exactly what she said. I left that medication in the medicine cabinet and never touched it again. But I wasn't out of the woods yet. I still felt horrible. I had been taking this concoction of antibiotics and none of them worked. It was a complete waste of my money and that doctor had no idea what he was talking about, just as I suspected.

I decided to see a gastroenterologist because my symptoms were getting worse. My stomach area was swelling and getting hard. I began vomiting daily and losing weight. I was short of breath, extremely fatigued, and very weak. On the way there, all I could think about was what could have caused all of this? Was it the grouper? I mean I was fine before I went to Destin and now I was sick as a dog! What the hell was this? Had someone poisoned me? Did someone put something in my drink when I wasn't looking?

I became paranoid and suspicious of everything and everyone. I was freaking out big time. When I arrived at the office, I noticed that I was the youngest person in the room. I began to feel out of place immediately. I felt like everyone was staring at me, the young guy, wondering what I was doing there.

I checked in at the front desk, took a seat, and waited for my name to be called. I began to doze off then, *voila,* my name was called. I walked to the back of the office and exchanged pleasantries with the nurse then proceeded to go into the doctor's office.

The nurse checked my vitals and noticed that my blood pressure was extremely elevated. She asked if I suffered from high blood pressure. I told her that I didn't. "I'm just nervous. Going to any doctor's office makes me nervous." She then asked me what I was there for and I began to explain all of my symptoms.

"Mr. Davis, that doesn't sound like a stomach issue to me at all," she said before checking my heartrate. She saw that it was extremely elevated as was my blood pressure. She asked me again if I had a problem with my heart. I told her, not to my knowledge. I'd never had heart issues of any kind. She asked if I'd ever had my heart checked before. I told her no. She recommended that I have my heart checked out immediately because my heartrate was too high.

The nurse left after that to see another patient and the doctor walked in. I explained the story all over again, but the doctor's theory was totally different from the nurse's. She told me that it was just an ulcer, which was the same thing I was told in South Carolina. She suggested that the antibiotic regimen that I stopped taking was too strong and that I should try this new "cocktail" as she called it. It was a combination of some other prescriptions that were supposed to help with the pain and get rid of the symptoms. I told her I had taken the cocktail regimen for several days, but to no avail, it didn't work either. I went to two different medical professionals and both misdiagnosed me as having a stomach issue.

I struggled with these symptoms for the remainder of January, basically confined to my house. I had zero energy to do anything or go anywhere. I felt depressed and I really thought I was going to die. I was watching myself deteriorate in front of my very eyes and there was nothing anyone could do to help me. I felt so helpless and full of despair.

February 2006 arrived and now I was living on fumes. So much so, I spent all of my days on my sofa in front of the TV frying my brain with all of the garbage that came on. I only got up to use the bathroom then I would sit right back down in front of the TV.

A friend of mine came over to check on me and noticed that my feet and ankles were swollen. "Johnnie, get up. I'm taking you to the hospital," she said. I didn't fuss this time, I had no energy to. I got dressed but noticed I had a problem. My ankles had swollen so much that I could not put on my shoes. I really hadn't noticed just how swollen my ankles got because I didn't wear shoes around the house. I was finally able to squeeze on an old pair of shoes and off to CMC Main Hospital in Charlotte we went. This day actually turned out to be a turning point in my life.

CHAPTER 3
MY GUARDIAN ANGEL

When I arrived at the hospital, I could not walk the full distance from the parking garage to the main entrance. Someone came to pick me up at the parking deck with a wheelchair and brought me inside. I remember bypassing everyone and not filling out any paperwork. A nurse came to me with a friendly, warm smile. "How are you feeling today, Mr. Davis?" she asked. I told her not good at all. She reassured me that they were going to fix me then began taking my vitals. Unlike my visit to the gastroenterologist, my heartrate was very low. It was so low that she struggled to find my pulse. The next thing I know, I had all of these white coats swarming around me and I was whisked away to some area of the hospital that looked odd to me for some reason. I was afraid, alone, and helpless, and my family was in New Jersey. I went from just moving to Charlotte a year ago, to now being in some strange section of the hospital in a room alone that reminded me of a scene from *X Files*. I was scared out of my mind.

Finally, someone came back to the room and drew blood from me. I asked if they knew what was going on and where the doctor was. The young lady who I assumed was a nurse, told me not to worry and that the doctor would be in to see me shortly. That was really code for the doctor will see you in about an hour or so.

A little over an hour later, the doctor came in. "Mr. Davis, we looked at the charts from your other doctor visits, and I can assure you, whatever the problem is it's surely not in your stomach. We want to keep you here for observation and we need to run some tests to determine what the cause of the problem is."

"So, you want to keep me here overnight?" I asked.

"Yes, you're in no condition to go home."

"Just how bad is it, doc? Am I going to die?"

"No, you're not going to die, but we can't let you go home just yet." I told him okay as I was in no position to fuss. I went through a battery of tests throughout the night. I was poked, prodded, x-rayed, you name it. I didn't get a wink of sleep at all.

And now I was here, sitting in Dr. Peters' office, eager to find out what was going on with my heart.

Dr. Peters looked at me in amazement. He said that I was lucky that my heart was in my body and not the body of a fifty-five-year-old man, otherwise I would most certainly be dead now. "You have no idea the danger you were in while traveling. You could have collapsed and died right where you were at any time!" He then asked if I was a believer. When I told him I was, he said that someone had their hand on me big time. He shook his head in amazement.

During my hospital stay, I met another doctor that really told it to me straight. I thought he was the coolest doctor in the hospital because he wore these awesome cowboy boots that I had never seen before. He walked up to my bedside.

"Mr. Davis. We tested you for everything and all of your blood-work is normal. We just can't seem figure out what caused your heart to fail."

He asked about my family history and I told him about my dad's death and that I didn't know of anyone having a heart condition on my mother's side of the family.

"Doc, what are my chances of survival? Will my heart return back to normal function?"

"Mr. Davis, you're young, so you have an excellent chance at survival. Your heart may go back to normal then again it may not. There's no sure-fire way to tell. I can tell you that you will get better, though." I asked him about the medication I was taking and wondered about the long-term side effects.

"That's a great question," he said, "and the answer is, I have no clue. There is no way to tell how these pills interact with each other and what the long-term side effects are in each patient. Our only hope is that we find the right combination of pills that will help do what we need them to do for you." I told him that I appreciated his honesty and candor. I really respected straight talk. He also mentioned that it would get worse for me before it got better. He advised me to hold on and tough it out. It was a painful process but he felt I was young enough to push through it.

I had no idea what he was talking about, though. I was safe and sound in the hospital surrounded by the best medical professionals in Charlotte, so I wasn't worried at all. Although my current situation was grim, my outlook was bright, and I looked forward to the day of walking out of the hospital and going home. Little did I know the true test was waiting for me.

As long as I was in that hospital setting, I felt secure and confident. As each day passed, I began to feel better and better. I was still very weak but at least the pain in my chest began to subside and I stopped vomiting. I told myself that I was going to somehow, someway, beat this. I kept repeating it over and over to bury it deep into my subconscious mind.

February 13, 2006, I was discharged from the hospital and was on my way home. My good friend and business associate,

Cindy, stayed with me the entire hospital stay and drove me back to my house. We worked together in our company and she knew that I didn't have any family to help me out during this time. I was extremely grateful because I had a long battle ahead of me. Without her being there, I doubt very seriously if I would have survived.

I could not wait to be home. There was no better feeling than being in my own house and sleeping in my own bed. No one coming into my room during the wee hours of the morning, poking me and drawing blood every two hours or so, was such a refreshing thought. It was impossible to get any rest in the hospital.

As I approached the door to go into the house, I had an incredibly weird feeling of anxiety come over me. For some reason, when I opened the door to go inside, the feeling of safety and security was no longer there and I immediately felt afraid. There were no doctors around or nurses, no one to watch me and make sure that I didn't slip into a coma or something. My stomach started feeling queasy. I walked into my bedroom and headed toward the bathroom. I made it as far as the sink and all of sudden my head began to spin. My heart started racing and I began to hyperventilate. I was having a panic attack! I panicked so much that I passed out in the bathroom.

The next thing I remember, I woke up in the hospital. Cindy was there and explained to me what happened. She told me that I passed out in the bathroom and that an ambulance came and picked me up and brought me to the hospital. I had no clue what happened. I was completely freaked out at this point!

After spending a few hours there, they determined that I was fine and I was released again. I went back home to try one more time. I put the key in the door and went inside. I walked in and noticed how everything smelled funny to me. It didn't feel like my house, it felt like I was someplace else. I walked to my bedroom, headed back to the bathroom and this time, I made it as far as the sink again. I looked up into the mirror and started sweating profusely. That queasy feeling returned to my stomach and I began to feel light-headed. My heart started racing and it felt like it was going to explode out of my chest for sure this time. I began hyperventilating again and boom! I passed out on the bathroom floor. I had another panic attack. Cindy drove me to the hospital and stayed with me again.

The nurses in the emergency room could not believe that I had come back twice in the same day! Apparently, I was suffering from separation anxiety from leaving a safe and secure environment to going to one that I no longer felt safe in. They kept me there for a few hours for observation and I was released. Before I actually left the hospital, the doctor pulled me to the side and said to me, "Mr. Davis, you can't keep doing this! You're going to be just fine. Now, if you want, I can write you a prescription for anxiety to help keep you calm, but I'd rather not do that because those pills are highly addictive. Besides, these visits to the emergency room aren't cheap. When you feel like you are going to pass out, take several deep breaths and just breathe. Keep doing that until you feel that fluttering in your chest start to fade away. You will be just fine. Pick your medication up from the pharmacy and start taking them immediately. More importantly, get some rest. Your body has been through a tremendous amount of stress and trauma."

I took his words to heart, no pun intended. I knew deep down inside that I had to find a way to pull it together because the monthly prescriptions along with the hospital fees, doctor fees, lab fees, and radiology fees, were all going to wipe out my savings. I'd saved quite a bit of money before leaving New Jersey, but I did not save anywhere near the amount I needed to pay off all of my medical expenses. I had no medical insurance and, at the time, could not qualify for charity care or anything of the sort because my business generated too much income. So, every last dime that I had was used to pay my medical bills and that was the beginning of something else to add onto the pile of crap that was happening in my life.

CHAPTER 4

THE ROAD TO RECOVERY

Mr. Davis, you're going to get worse before you get better, was the only thing I heard over and over in my head by Dr. Cowboy Boots. The road to recovery was extremely painful and arduous to say the least. My first few days home alone, I thought I was surely going to die. I was so afraid to go to sleep because I didn't think I was going to wake up. I was taking eighteen different pills per day and not sleeping. Can you say delirious, not to mention heavily medicated? That was not a good combination anywhere on earth.

After two days of not sleeping, I really began to go haywire. I was paranoid, tired, weak, and in severe pain. My liver was enlarged because my internal organs began to shut down, which was the source of the severe pain I felt in my stomach area. My heart wasn't able to pump the blood throughout my body efficiently, causing me to retain fluid in my lower extremities. I developed a pot belly from the enlarged liver and retained over forty pounds of fluid. I was unable to urinate frequently due to the fluid buildup. My kidneys were failing since I was unable to urinate. I was a complete wreck. I began to feel sorry for myself big time and asked God over and over, why me? What had I done to deserve this?

I would talk to my friends back in New Jersey and everyone would say the same thing. God has a plan for you. God is going to heal you. Just keep praying. Everything happens for a reason.

I have to be honest, I didn't want to hear any more of that talk. I just wanted to get well. I needed someone to tell me what to do to help myself get better. Give me the magic pill, potion, something other than just a prayer or two. I needed some relief from this personal hell I was living in, and at the time, prayer alone was taking too long. Have you ever been in a situation where you needed relief from a severe physical and/or emotional pain, and the only thing it seemed that people offered you was prayer? However well-intentioned, it just didn't seem like enough.

Nightfall came and I forced myself to stay awake because I was too afraid to go to sleep. I picked up the bible and began to read the book of Job. While reading the first chapter, I looked away for a second and fixed my eyes on the coffee table in front of me. I saw three little demons the size of elves pointing at me, repeating, "You're going to die! You're going to die," and I actually froze in my seat.

This isn't real, I said to myself. *I'm just tired and delirious from not sleeping in almost three days. I'm not crazy. My mind is playing tricks on me.* I put the bible down and closed it. As soon as I did, the demons vanished into thin air. There was no way I could explain what just happened to me. I mean, who would believe something like that? That sounds too crazy.

I picked myself up off the sofa and walked into the kitchen to get some water. I was still in disbelief as to what happened in the living room. I began to wonder if the house was haunted or something. Was I high? Had I crossed over into the spirit realm somehow? Did I imagine what I had seen? I had so many questions, but no one to ask. I just threw my hands up and said, oh, what the hell. Whatever's going to happen will happen. I had reached a point where the fatigue set in from not sleeping and I no longer cared if I woke up or not. I came to the conclusion that it was out of my control and I needed to get some rest.

I was determined not to become fear's whipping boy and I repeated to myself over and over that I was not going to worry about it, nor would I be afraid. I sat down on the sofa and fell asleep. I think I must have slept for twelve hours straight because when I awoke, it was bright and early the next day. The sun was shining and I said to myself, "I made it! I'm blessed to see another day, so let's see what this day brings." I guess prayer does actually work sometimes in the most mysterious ways.

I received a call from my mother and it was so good to hear her warm, loving voice. She told me that she and my sister were going to come and stay with me for a week or so to help me out. They wanted to make sure that I was doing okay. My voice was rather weak from all the trauma, but I told her to come on down and that I would love to see them.

They caught the Amtrak train from New Jersey and it seemed like it took forever for them to arrive. That's probably because it did actually; the ride was thirteen hours. I was so excited to see my family, it was like Christmas all over again. I arranged for Cindy to drive my car to pick my mother and sister up from the train station. Although I was happy to see them, I had no energy to get out of the car to greet them. It was too cold and I was too weak to make that kind of a move, so I sat there and watched them put their bags in the car.

They both got in and we drove back to my house. I remember the first time my mom laid eyes on me, she looked like she wanted to cry. She had never seen me look like this. I didn't look like the son she had just seen a month ago. My health had deteriorated fast.

During the ride home, we spoke about what transpired with me and all of the details leading up to the event of my hospital stay. I can remember only wanting to sleep and not talk at all; I was so exhausted. My mom sat in the backseat right behind me and I can remember her rubbing my head, telling me that it was going to be alright. She rubbed my head all the way home and I immediately turned into the eight-year-old boy that felt safe to have my mother there with me. Everyone knows that moms make everything better, right? As she rubbed my head, I began to repeat silently to myself that I was going to be alright.

We finally arrived at my house about thirty minutes later and it was a struggle to get out of the car. I mean, it literally took every ounce of strength I could muster to walk from the garage to the kitchen, which was only a few feet away. I could not believe how miserable I was feeling but I was trying my best not to display it. I did not want my mother to start freaking out. I couldn't bear to see my mother's tears because that would have destroyed me. So, I sucked it up and walked inside the house and went straight to the sofa. All I wanted to do was rest.

My sister came and sat next to me and we talked for a few minutes. She told me about the colorful characters they saw on the train and what they were doing. We laughed and joked about it and it felt good. She really lifted my spirits and at that moment I appreciated her for doing that. Anyone that knows me knows that I love to laugh and joke around. But as of late, I was not in a laughing or joking mood. I began slipping into this dark space of misery and despair. I felt so helpless, like I may have been a burden on someone for the rest of my life. The mere thought of that made me depressed.

After a while, we gathered in the living room and talked about what my plans were for the future. I shared with my mother what the doctors had told me regarding my recovery process and everything I had to do. I had to take approximately fourteen pills per day and adhere to a very low sodium diet. Walking was encouraged if I could do it, but at this stage since it was my second week home from the hospital, all I had to do was take my medication and rest.

After we finished catching up, I turned in and called it a night. That small amount of entertaining was exhausting. Cindy stayed with us as well. She wanted to make sure that I was going to be okay. After all, if anything were to happen, she knew exactly where to go and what to do. My mother and sister were visitors to Charlotte and didn't know how to navigate the city.

I went to bed but could not fall asleep right away. The thought kept coming to mind, *what if you don't wake up? What if your heart stops? Who's going to hear it?* I thought that maybe I should stay up for a while longer because this could very well be the last time I saw my family. I had all of these thoughts racing through my head. I then began feeling like I was going to have another panic attack. My chest started hurting and I was feeling short of breath. I knew that I was causing this with my thinking because while we were all talking in the living room, I was fine.

I remembered what the doctor told me to do whenever I started to feel like I was having an attack. I shut my eyes and took several deep breaths. After a while, the shortness of breath stopped and I was able to finally fall asleep. But I had terrible nightmares almost every night. I mean horror movie kind of nightmares where someone was trying to kill me or I was being chased. I had nightmares of me fighting two and three people at a time. My body was bloody from fighting and I was running for my life. These types of nightmares occurred seemingly every night making me not want to go to sleep. I thought maybe it was a side effect from the medication I was taking. I was heavily medicated and I remember Dr. Cowboy Boots telling me that he had no clue how all of the medication would interact with each other. So, I decided to do a little investigating on my own. I took out my lap top and began to research the medication I was taking. I could not believe the laundry list of side effects from each one of the pills. I became even more afraid of the medication than I was my actual heart condition. I was really in a quandary because the medication I was taking to help me was the same medication causing me to feel like I was losing my mind at times.

Some of the side effects I experienced were: extreme fatigue, brain fog, metallic taste in my mouth, blurred vision, restlessness, and over production of saliva. For some odd reason, I could not stop spitting out saliva. It was as if I was a tobacco chewer or snuff user. I also experienced depression, anxiety, and days when I just felt like I had been knocked over the head with a sledge hammer. I don't know the medical term for the "knocked over the head by a sledge hammer" reference, but just imagine someone hitting you over the head with one. Would you really care about what it was called? I tried to explain all of this to my mother and she just did what any southern born-again mother would do, she broke out her bible and began to pray for me.

My mother was also the queen of natural home remedies, so she took it upon herself to do her own research and suggested I take her to the grocery store. It was early afternoon and I told her I was in no condition to drive. But she could drive my car and I would tell her where to go. We went to the Whole Foods super market and she purchased all of the ingredients she needed to make this special juice that was going to help me with the digestion issue I was having. When she came back to the car, I didn't ask what items she had purchased. I could clearly see there were a lot of green vegetables.

We made it back to my house and she began to take out the mystery items that were going to help me. I saw parsley, cabbage, spinach, green beans, and something that appeared to be ginger root. "Mom, I can't take ginger," I told her. "It's a stimulant even if it's all natural." I was taking this nasty highly-toxic prescription called Amiodarone and it was super strong. The drug was designed to slow my heartrate down so that it did not beat out of rhythm. Ginger Root would counteract that and I was not looking forward to going back to the hospital anytime soon.

Out came the juicer and in went the parsley, cabbage, spinach, etc. It was the most horrible smell of vegetables I had ever smelled in my life. The scent of the juice almost caused me to vomit. There was absolutely no way I was going to drink that. My mom insisted but I vehemently declined. "Mom, I love you but this smells horrible and I bet it tastes equally as bad, yuck!" She didn't say a word, she just stood there as if to say, "I'll wait. Are you done?"

After I finished drinking this God-awful concoction, I sat down for a moment and just waited. Sure enough, after a few minutes, I vomited it all up. I reverted back to my childhood days and said, "See Mom, I told you! Are you happy now?" Not only did I feel horrible but now my breath stank, too! Boy, was I having a rough day. There was nothing worse than having a weakened heart and bad breath.

I didn't have much of an appetite, so eating became a chore. This was so ironic because I always enjoyed a good meal. I was never overweight or had any type of eating disorder, I just loved to eat a delicious meal, and now it was a struggle. My energy was at an all-time low and I honestly did not know what I was going to do going forward. I was thirty-four years old and I had come to a serious crossroad in my life. I had some real soul searching to do because every article that I read about congestive heart failure was not all encouraging.

My prognosis was not looking good. Every medical journal that I read stated that the likelihood of a full recovery was slim and that the lifespan of a congestive heart failure patient was not long. To be honest, it was rather depressing to read all of this information. The more I searched for something to give me an ounce of hope, the more I found there was nothing promising.

I referenced back to the conversation that I had with the cardiologist about what could have caused this. I kept hearing Idiopathic Cardiomyopathy ringing in my head over and over again and it would not go away. I became obsessed with discovering what happened to me and how I could have prevented this. I went through a series of emotions but the one that stuck out the most was anger.

I was upset that this happened to me. I was also upset that the doctors could not tell me why or how I could fix it. How could this have happened to me in the prime of my life when everything seemed to be going so well? I thought God was playing a cruel joke on me and I really had no answers.

I began to retrace my life steps, starting from the beginning. I had all kinds of questions going back to high school. Did I feel anything then? Did I notice any fluttering in my chest while playing basketball or football? Was I ever short of breath and just ignored it? I didn't smoke, never took any illegal drugs a day in my life and had never been a big drinker by any stretch of the imagination, so what on earth could have caused this? These were just some of the questions that ran through my mind daily as I tried to rationalize why this happened to me. The more questions I had, the more the answers seemed to escape me. And because I had no answers, I became even more frustrated because I have always been a problem solver.

Throughout my professional career, I had the honor of studying under some of the most brilliant minds in the area of personal development and leadership. I've taught these success principles to thousands of people and have always had an answer to help solve any situation. But this time, I had no answers and it put me in a place of uncertainty, a place where I prided myself on never being.

I learned years ago that if you want to get better answers you have to ask better questions. So, instead of focusing on what happened and how this happened, I decided to turn my attention to how to defeat congestive heart failure. I began asking different questions pertaining to improving my heart function and improving my overall quality of life, and with that came empowering answers.

This is a technique that I learned from my personal development studies which proved to be very effective in helping me to attract the key people in my life that enabled me to create so much success in business. It's a principle that I believed would be just as effective in this situation. I was living with the problem, so I was very aware of what that was. Now I needed a solution. I shifted my focus to asking how I could reclaim my health. What was required of me to regain my strength?

I became consumed with doing everything possible to get better. I didn't have the time or the energy to feel sorry for myself anymore. Slowly but surely, my health started to improve and I began to regain my strength. The first thing I did was make sure I stuck to my low sodium, heart-healthy diet and I eliminated as much junk as possible. That meant no fried foods of any kind, foods high in cholesterol or trans fats. I also went back to the gym and started working out regularly. I hired a trainer for the accountability aspect. I never needed one in the past, but I figured I would try something different this time and take things up a notch. Besides, I knew if I ever felt tempted to slack off at any moment, my trainer would push me which is exactly what I needed.

I repeated affirmations to myself every morning without fail. I told myself that I was completely healthy and that my heart was healed and normal. I would stare into the mirror and say it over and over again with passion and emotion. I needed to really bury this new thought deep into my subconscious mind because I knew the road ahead was going to be tough and there were going to be days when I just didn't feel like doing anything. One of the key things I stopped doing was going to support group meetings. I attended two of them but quickly realized they were not the place for me. All I heard were sad stories of how people literally destroyed their health with their harsh lifestyles and I couldn't relate to any of them. I didn't want to hear their negative pity-filled stories and I did not want to fill my subconscious with it either.

Although I was nowhere near close to being 100%, it was a step in the right direction. I was able to move around more and get out of the house and run small errands. I felt like I was getting back on track and I felt a sense of normalcy returning; I was so empowered by that. I was able to take care of myself and I didn't need Cindy to help me do everything like before. This was great for her because she had her own life to get back to. I was really grateful to have her in my life at that time because, like I mentioned earlier, I don't think I would have survived without her being there.

After Cindy left, she continued to check on me from time to time. The biggest "win" was that I had completely overcome my fear of being alone and worrying about not waking up when I fell asleep. The nightmares were subsiding and I was able to get a good night's sleep. For the first time in a long time, I felt confident that I would return back to my normal self in no time. I asked myself the empowering questions daily and my mind went to work on finding the solutions. I was solution-oriented and stopped being problem focused. However, while my attitude shifted toward the brighter side of things and my health was getting better, little did I know that there were other challenges lurking in the shadows that I hadn't even considered.

CHAPTER 5

I WAS TOTALLY UNPREPARED

As a self-employed independent business owner, I enjoyed the freedom that came along with it. I was not under the thumb of a boss and I had complete autonomy over my time and income. The one area that I wish I was more proactive in was taking care of was my health insurance. I can recall hearing my mother telling me to take care of that immediately after I relocated to Charlotte and I always put it off. I was usually pretty thorough when it came to insurance matters because that's where I began my corporate professional career.

My first real job out of college was working in the Health Insurance industry with a Fortune 500 insurance company back in 1994. I always had benefits and knew the importance of having them because one catastrophic illness or injury could wipe your finances clean if you didn't have something in place. Back then, I never once thought about it. I hardly went to the doctor except to get my annual check-up, but that was about it. It wasn't until I left the health insurance industry in 2003 to become an independent business owner, that I realized how important it was. For years, I didn't have it and I was playing Russian roulette with my health-care; with my life for that matter. I never took into consideration the cost of paying for insurance on my own. I could easily afford it but I guess I was being cheap and didn't want to spend the extra money on something I hardly used when I did have it. That was the absolute stupidest logic I ever could have convinced myself of. I charge it to being young, naïve, and just plain dumb. I knew better but still did not act on it. That was the worst decision I could have ever made.

From December 2005 through February 2006, everything that could go wrong with my health and finances certainly did, and it all happened at the same time. I had saved quite a bit of money before leaving New Jersey for North Carolina and I had some big plans. I had everything all laid out perfectly. I was going to continue building my sales team in my old company and I was going to also become a Real Estate Investor. My plan was to become a multi-millionaire in real estate and travel the world, get married, and live happily ever after. Well, the complete opposite happened and things began to unravel quickly.

Because I didn't have health insurance, I had to pay for every doctor's visit, prescription, lab fee, x-ray, and hospital charge out of pocket, and these bills were huge! It did not take long for my savings to be wiped clean from just the hospital charges alone. My prescriptions were approximately six hundred dollars per month because I was taking so many. I became afraid to go to my mailbox because I knew it was filled with bills, bills, and more bills! It was enough to actually cause a heart attack for sure.

Gone were my real estate investing dreams and hello to paying off all of my medical bills because I just could not bear to see the sight of them. While I was paying off my medical expenses, my business began to dwindle because I wasn't able to give it the attention that it required each month, and things were getting tighter and tighter in my house. I was in a serious conundrum because I physically did not have the strength to go and get a regular job nor could my heart tolerate the stress. I was feeling better and getting stronger, but I wasn't strong enough to get back to work. Besides, I didn't want to go back into the work force. I busted my ass to leave Corporate America and I had no desire whatsoever to return to it. But I had no clue what I was going to do.

I was alive though I couldn't say that I was living. Due to the additional financial stress, my health took a turn for the worse and I felt overwhelmed with everything. I can't think of a worse combination than being physically sick and drowning in medical bills with no foreseeable help.

I remember sitting on the couch, hyperventilating for no apparent reason. I thought for sure that this was the "big one". I was alone in my house and my thoughts just took a negative turn. I got to a point where I felt so beat up that I just couldn't take it anymore. In an instant I went from hyperventilating to sobbing like a baby. I fell down on my knees and lay face-down on my living room floor and asked God to heal me or take me because I couldn't do it anymore. I gave up. I wanted to live but I didn't want to live like this and my health had improved, but only slightly. My technique of asking empowering questions seemed to take a backseat. I really felt that it was easier for me and for everyone around me if I just died in my sleep. I wouldn't feel any more pain, I wouldn't owe anymore bills, and all of this misery would be over. I never thought about how my friends and family would miss me. I just wanted the pain to go away. I laid there crying alone and eventually fell asleep right on the floor. I don't remember what time it was. All I remember is waking up to daylight outside and I was famished.

My first thought was that this was a good sign. My appetite had returned. I picked myself up off the floor and went to the bathroom to wash my face and brush my teeth. I stared in the mirror and just looked at how miserable my appearance was. I really didn't like the person I saw in the mirror. I hadn't cut my hair in weeks, maybe even over a month. I never left the house to go anywhere other than to sneak to the mailbox occasionally, or take a ride to the post office.

I decided right then and there I was going to change that. I took out my clippers and cut all of my hair off and gave myself a bald head. I also cut off all of my facial hair and said I was going to start anew, which began with a new look. Something happened to me between the time I asked God to heal me or take me and that day because I woke up with an energy and zeal that I hadn't had before.

My physical body had undergone a significant change as well. My stomach was swollen and I retained an enormous amount of fluid in my body because my heart was not functioning at full capacity. My stamina was still very low, but despite all that, something transformed in me spiritually and mentally because I didn't care how I looked. I referred back to my technique of asking empowering questions. I began to focus 100% on getting well again. So, everything that I did from that day forward was in an effort to get well. I changed my physical state by implementing a power move technique that I learned from the master coach Tony Robbins. He talked about changing your physiology by first changing your physical state. Walking around, yelling, dancing, chanting, clapping anything you could do to interrupt a pattern of negative thinking could change your state of mind.

Before I shaved my head and face clean, I played the theme music from the movie *Rocky* and began shadow boxing in the mirror. My favorite line from the movie was when he said the toughest opponent you will ever face in the ring is yourself. I was in a championship boxing match with healthy Johnnie Davis and sick Johnnie Davis. The battle wasn't just physical, it was 90% mental. I knew that I couldn't lose the mental battle, because if I did, the physical was lost, too, and that's when you really needed to hang things up. I wasn't ready to hang up my gloves just yet.

I prayed more than I ever did before and had some serious conversations with God. I was talking to him as though he were sitting right next to me in my house. He certainly had my complete and undivided attention. As each day passed, I felt better and better. The medications were starting to kick in finally.

I suppose a non-believer would say this is a bunch of rubbish. They'd say, "You mean to tell me that you spoke with this imaginary being and had conversations with Him as if you were actually talking to another human being and things just got better for you?" And my response would be, yes. That's exactly what happened and I choose to believe that me speaking to God enabled me to receive the message that I was looking for which was a feeling of intense positivity. This feeling put me on the pathway to healing because this is what I truly desired in my heart. It was something that I chose to believe then and I still choose to believe it today.

Some would say it was the medications, Johnnie. You said it yourself, they started to kick in and that's why you felt better. I would say that's true, however, I had always taken my meds, but this time it was different. I truly believed that I was going to be fine; I had this overwhelming feeling of calm and peace. I had never experienced that feeling before.

By this time, it was now June 2006 and summer had just started. I felt my energy beginning to increase and my cardiologist found the right combination of medication for me to get the results we had both hoped for. One of the medications I was taking at the time was called Furosemide. It was a diuretic designed to help remove excess fluid from the body. Some people refer to it as "a water pill". I had to get a higher dosage of that one because of the excess fluid buildup in my body. Within one week, I urinated out thirty pounds of fluid and my dry weight was 178 pounds. I went from 208 pounds to 178 pounds in one week and that was a scary sight to see. I had no idea I lost so much muscle mass and was carrying so much fluid. The past few months of not eating much had finally revealed what was really there. I hadn't weighed 178 pounds since the eighth grade. Needless to say, none of my clothes fit and I had to start over again.

Once again, I said to myself, *Johnnie, you can beat this. Let's take it one day at a time.* First things first, I had to get some food! I began to season all of my food with Mrs. Dash seasoning and it was actually pretty good. I went on an eating binge—healthy foods, of course—and I even began walking in my neighborhood just to build up my endurance. Slowly but surely, I began to feel stronger and stronger and my health was improving! My business was still dwindling but at least I could now walk around the corner and back! I learned quickly to celebrate the small victories. I told myself that I would never take something so simple as walking around the corner and back for granted ever again because not everyone can do it. You don't appreciate small things like that until you can no longer do them.

While my strength increased, my business continued to disappear and I watched my income shrink month by month as the bills poured in, not to mention living expenses. Someone at the doctor's office mentioned possibly applying for disability because of my low ejection fraction. The ejection fraction is the measurement of how much your heart squeezes blood throughout the body. A normal ejection fraction is between 55-70% according to most experts in the field of cardiology. My ejection fraction at the time was in the high teens which was not good even though I felt like I was getting better. I never thought about Disability and I despised the thought of being categorized as someone that may be disabled or in need of government assistance. As an entrepreneur, it went against my entire belief system of self-reliance.

After a long discussion with who else, my mom again, I decided to see what would I qualify for, if anything. As it would turn out, I qualified for disability because of low ejection fraction. However, because I was thirty-four years old at the time, they felt that I was young enough to make a full recovery, so the chances of me actually receiving disability was long shot. Despite the odds, I applied anyway. And, of course, I was denied. I was so annoyed at the fact that I was denied because not only was I against Disability in the first place, they actually denied me. I thought to myself, if I had absolutely no income right now, I would be S.O.L! I walked out of the office feeling like the system was a scam and that they make you jump through hoops just to get a few pennies. I left there more determined than ever to figure out a way to get things going in the right direction again. I was confident that a solution would present itself. It was just a matter of being patient and waiting for the right opportunity. Little did I know, that opportunity was right around the corner.

CHAPTER 6

PATIENCE IS A VIRTUE

The next day, I had a conversation with a friend regarding a serious real estate investment opportunity down in Atlanta, Georgia that was a real slam dunk. She explained to me how the real estate market was so robust that the banks were practically giving money away to people that had excellent credit. She told me how I could qualify for a no document loan with stellar credit and get just about anything I wanted. This was music to my ears because my business was failing and I needed money in the worst way. I fell in love with the idea that was presented before me and decided to take a chance. Why not capitalize on what appeared to be a homerun of a deal?

In November of 2006, I drove to Georgia to take a look at the available property and to meet with the builder and project manager that was going to oversee the construction of the new house. It was a lake front property in a beautiful gated community. I was completely blown away. The lot size was perfect and it was available at a steal of a price. It didn't take long for me to jump all over it because I understood what was at stake. The potential profit after constructions costs and repaying the bank was $275,000! I thought that all of my troubles with my heart lead me to such a great opportunity. I said to myself, *thank you, God, for making a way when there was no other way.* I believed that my money troubles would be over with this one deal and I could finally get back on track with my life and focus on improving my health.

We all drove over to the bank and I began filling out all of the paperwork to get the loan processed. After checking my credit, the loan officer told me I had excellent credit and that it was going to be a pleasure doing business with me. I thought that was rather odd for him to point that out, but I didn't say anything. I just smiled, thanked him, and continued signing my life away to secure the loan for the lot and to start building the house.

Once the paperwork was complete, the loan officer congratulated me and told me I was officially a Georgia land owner! I thought to myself, *what an amazing day!* My heart was getting stronger each day and now I was about to build a house in Georgia. In eight months, all of my money troubles would be over! I was on cloud nine heading back to Charlotte, thinking about how awesome things were going to be.

We broke ground in December 2006 on the house and I was extremely excited because all I could think about was that in August 2007 everything was going to be alright. This was the scheduled date of completion on the house and I couldn't wait. I celebrated Christmas on a high note. Yet, a few short weeks later, we were into the new year and there was all this talk about the "real estate bubble bursting" and predatory lending. I was totally thrown for a loop but I held onto hope that I could make the project work. But then we ran into a few hiccups with securing the permits needed to begin construction on the house, which caused major delays.

Finally, after weeks of waiting, we attained the proper permits, only to discover that the ground was frozen solid, making it difficult to dig into the ground to pour the foundation. Once we finally worked through that, things began to move along until the house was 65% complete. Around March of 2007, everything literally went south. It was as if time itself stopped and we hit a wall. I was receiving calls from contractors and subcontractors stating that they hadn't received payment for services rendered which took me for a loop.

My partner at the time was the project manager who was overseeing the project. I discovered that she was mismanaging the funds and was using the house money for personal reasons unbeknownst to me. I was so pissed at her! I trusted her because she came highly recommended by someone I really respected and she knew I was not in the best of health. I never in my life felt so betrayed by a friend. It was my fault because I should have been more on top of things.

Companies were going out of business left and right. The cement company folded, so did the window company. It was a serious domino effect of companies falling one right after the other. Even the bank that processed my loan went out of business! The builder decided to skip town and head back to California never to be heard from again! In the meantime, I received calls from everyone under the sun asking me for payment for this service or that service and my business partner decided not to answer any of my calls! Can you say stressed out? My heart was racing every day and I was suffering from anxiety once again. I don't like to use the word hate because it's so strong of a word, but I hated the lurch that my business partner put me in. When I think about it today, I still have a nasty taste in my mouth.

The next several months had to be the most stressful period in my adult life. I had never had my phone ring so much from so many different people asking me for money that I did not have to pay. I didn't know what I was going to do. My heart was still healing but the stress was just too overwhelming. I had many sleepless nights and wondered if my heart would eventually give out. I did my best not to focus on it and applied my power move techniques to change my state of mind. But the phone calls kept coming and it was a rather challenging situation to contend with. I felt like I was alone and that I had no one to turn to. I was reminded of the old adage that if it sounds too good to be true, it probably is. This was one deal that I wish I would have exercised a little more patience and sought advice from someone that could have given me a heads-up on the state of the real estate market. This is one example of why it pays to have mentors in different fields.

Thank God I was able to connect with a real estate investor in Georgia that agreed to do a short sale on the property. All of the contractors and subcontractors that were looking for payment eventually settled for the agreed payments and all was good again. I did not achieve my end goal of building the house and selling it for $275,000 profit, but I did gain something that was even more priceless: my peace of mind. My phone stopped ringing with creditors and contractors looking to get paid and my heart palpitations decreased from all of the intense financial stress that I was under. But despite all of the hardship, I learned some valuable lessons for the future.

The first one was never do business with "friends". Everything sounds great until something goes awry. Number two, don't make decisions under emotional duress because, in most cases, you're probably not thinking clearly. Now, I had no idea that the real estate market was going to crash when it did. However, had I done just a little more research and consulted with more experienced investors, perhaps they would have spared me the headache of going through that process.

In a sick and twisted way, I'm kind of grateful that I did go through it because it added to my life experience belt. When it was all said and done, I really hadn't lost any additional money. It was all the bank's money and the other contractors. Sure, it cost me time, aggravation, and stress like you wouldn't believe, but one thing is absolutely certain; I will never do it again. I choose my business partners more wisely now. I've learned to surround myself with mentors and people that have more knowledge in certain areas of business, life, etc., and glean their wisdom. Once wisdom enters your heart, and knowledge is pleasant to your soul, it will keep you from all hurt, harm, and danger.

CHAPTER 7

THE TURNING POINT

In the beginning of 2008, I decided that this year was going to be my year. I was going to turn it all around and get things going in high gear again. My heart function improved significantly but it was still in a weakened state. My ejection fraction reached a high of 39% which, although still low, was high enough for me to be fully functional. I was going to the gym regularly and doing cardio and light weight training. I was able to pick my sales business back up and gain some traction. I had to start all over again but it was what I had done for the past seven years and I was good at it. I was an ancillary benefits specialist marketing Legal Service plans and Identity Theft protection for individuals, small business and corporate accounts. I built a sales force of over 10,000 people across the country. I also trained and did motivational speaking engagements as well and I really loved what I was doing at that time. It afforded me the opportunity to work on my own time and at my own pace, which came in handy during my recovery period. Once I was able to get back in the marketplace, I believed that I could turn things around.

During this time, I was investigating new remedies and new products that I could use to help strengthen my heart function.

I still could never get "idiopathic cardiomyopathy" out of my mind nor could I accept the doctor's answer of "we don't know what caused this to happen to you." I went back to researching everything I could find from supplements, juices, special diets, vitamins, herbs, you name it. I tried them all and, although some of them were good products, I still never achieved the results that I was looking to accomplish, which was a higher ejection fraction.

I met with Naturopaths, Chiropractors, and other alternative healthcare professionals to see if we could come up with something that would help me. I attended a few heart failure support group meetings again to see what new information I could gather from others there. Maybe I would hear something that I hadn't heard or researched so far. I thought it was worth trying.

I went to the first meeting and noticed I was the youngest person there. I was immediately annoyed with that because I still couldn't accept the fact that I was dealing with this. I sat down and listened to what sounded like endless complaining about who was feeling the worst, and who was taking the most medication. In my mind, it was tantamount to hearing babies at a nursery crying uncontrollably, and I wanted to bolt out of the room so badly. We were all sitting around the round table, introducing ourselves and sharing what caused our heart issues. I heard everything from overdosing on cocaine, complications from diabetes, intravenous drug usage, complications from obesity, smoking, and I couldn't believe my ears. I didn't engage in any of those things and I was never overweight, let alone obese, so I just couldn't understand how I got in this predicament. When my name was called, I was asked to share.

"Hi, my name is Johnnie Davis and I'm thirty-six years old. My diagnosis was idiopathic cardiomyopathy and I have no idea how that happened. I'm not a heavy drinker, I don't smoke, and I've never used any illegal drugs ever in my life. I don't have diabetes and, as you can see, I'm not overweight. I'm trying to figure out how I can improve my heart function from this point forward."

The doctor in the room spoke first. "There is nothing we can give you to improve the function of your heart per se. You all take medication and it's designed to decrease your chances of arrhythmia and such. However, improved heart function will have to occur by what you do in terms of your nutrition and exercise, and, of course, taking your meds as prescribed." After he finished speaking, I figured I could leave. I had gotten the answer I was looking for. *I'm definitely in the wrong place,* I thought to myself. I decided that I wasn't sick and I was not going to put myself in environments like this. I was going to go where healthy people go and do the things that healthy people do.

I turned my attention to the world of naturopathic healing because the more information I discovered about minerals and nutrients, the more it spoke to how important nutrition was in helping the body heal itself. This proved to be more prophetic later on in my life. I decided to completely change my diet and give organic living a try.

Now, my diet wasn't poor before by any means; however, I figured that making this change could only help. I spoke with my dietician and she gave me a list of things to avoid and foods that I should eat daily. Of course, I started with the basics, eating organic fruit and vegetables and eliminating as much sugar from my diet as possible, the fake sugars and artificial sweeteners in particular. I switched to eating more fish such as wild caught salmon and cod baked or grilled, and I avoided all fried foods and no fast food of any kind. I didn't consume alcohol and my sodium intake was just at the daily allowance. I continued to season my food with Mrs. Dash because it's made without sodium and is what my dietician recommended. My cardiomyopathy was not related to my diet but it was part of the "heart healthy" protocol to stick to this recommended way of eating. In addition to this, I exercised three to four times a week. My workouts included some weight training and cardio. I usually walked on the treadmill for thirty minutes or so, nothing too strenuous.

My ejection fraction was in the low thirties at this point, so there was only so much that I could physically do. However, I pushed myself to the limit whenever I could. Some days were better than others pertaining to my strength and stamina. At times, I just didn't make it because I was physically drained. My mind was willing to go the distance but my body said, "Park it right here, buddy." This was my routine for the most part. I resented the fact that I had to take a nap during the day because I thought that was something that senior citizens did. I was only thirty-six years old. I shouldn't have to take naps midday.

I have to say that I was the quintessential example of a person in extreme denial. I would never admit that I had cardiomyopathy and I would never utter the words "heart disease". To me this was a freak situation that would eventually correct itself and I would bounce back because I was strong. All of my years of personal development training taught me that I created my own reality with my thoughts and that I could change my situation with feeding my mind positive information and keeping my attitude positive at all times. Besides, this was something I taught my sales team for years and I watched many of them blossom into top income producers. The one thing I didn't consider was the fact that coaching your team on how to become better in their lives was one thing, but talking to yourself about overcoming heart failure was something entirely different.

The one thing I longed for more than anything else was for someone to understand exactly what I was going through but without pity. I needed people that were positive, highly motivated, and encouraging because there were many dark days where I just didn't know what was going to happen. I experienced a lot of confusion at times and I knew it was the side effects of some of the medication I was taking. One day, I was fired up and ready to take on the world, and other days I didn't want to leave the house. All of the information that I read about people with cardiomyopathy indicated that the long-term prognosis wasn't too promising. It was actually scary to read that I may not live past fifty years old and that my quality of life was going to be terrible going forward. I would never be able to live my life as I once did with the energy, vigor, and mental clarity, but, instead, be filled with endless doctor's appointments and lifelong medications with God only knows what kinds of long-term side effects on other parts of my body. It was really depressing and I knew the more I stayed in my own head and continued reading stuff like that, the more likely I may have to battle depression along with my heart ailment and I just did not want to go down that dangerous path. I knew people that were taking medication for depression and for their heart and they were in really bad shape mentally and physically.

One day, I decided to call my good friends, Tremaine and Pastor George, because these guys were not only men of God, they were my business partners and friends and I thoroughly enjoyed talking with both of them. They always knew exactly what to say and how to say it to me. They gave me the tough love that I needed whenever I started feeling sorry for myself. I got both of them on the phone and we chatted away about everything from business to politics because we had our first African American presidential candidate running for office during this time.

I shared with them that I wasn't really feeling 100% and then gave them a laundry list of what was wrong with me. I started the conversation off by telling them how lethargic I felt, not quite short of breath, but my breathing was a little off, etc. I could just imagine Tremaine over the phone playing the imaginary violin as I continued talking. He's an ex-football player and coach and has the compassion of a Navy Seal, but he's still a great friend nonetheless.

Finally, after a few minutes of me rambling on my woe-is-me soap box, Tremaine interrupted me. "Hey, man, we hear what you're saying, but we have one question. What are you going to do about it? Aren't you the one that taught us to be solution-oriented instead of problem focused? It sounds like you're focusing more on what is going wrong with you instead of what's right. If you're going to continue singing your sad song, you're going to have to do it by yourself. But before we let you go, Pastor George will say a prayer for you." I said to myself, "Gee, thanks, fellas. You're all heart!"

Pastor George began to pray over the phone and I just listened with my eyes closed. His words were so soothing because I really needed to hear the encouragement; that God did not bring me this far to leave me hanging. I thanked both of them for spending that precious time with me and we hung up the phone.

That one conversation taught me a valuable lesson and I never called anyone again with my sad story. Your friends and even your Pastor don't want to hear or be bogged down with your problems. I had to laugh after a while because, for some reason, it was just so funny. I totally did not expect the call to go that way but I was grateful that it did. They kindly gave me the swift kick in the butt that I needed to get out of my funk.

At that point, I had a choice to make. Either get busy living or get busy dying. Either way, I was going to be busy doing something. I chose to get busy living and I made a commitment to go on and become as healthy and as strong as I possibly could. I read every self-help personal development book I could get my hands on because I learned early on in my career that everything stems from your thoughts. Your thoughts are things and if I could inundate my mind with positivity and empowering information, I could create the outcome I desired. I talked to God more than I ever had in my life and we really had some serious conversations. I guess that's what people describe as soul searching. I had to come up with my game plan for the future and change a lot of what I was doing.

The first genius idea I had was to not only research the medication I was on in great detail to look at the side effects, but also find a way of somehow getting to a point where I could actually come off of the medications altogether. The more research I did on the medicines, the more alarmed I became at the possible long-term effects they would have on my brain, kidneys, liver, and heart. I had to find a way to get off these poisons!

At my next doctor's appointment, I spoke with my cardiologist about coming off of my medications at some point in time. He looked at me in total astonishment. I will never forget the look on his face when I first brought it up. He said to me, "You're not serious, are you? Do you realize that just two years ago, you were twenty-four hours away from expiring? Your heart is still relatively weak. Although you are asymptomatic for the most part, I'm afraid these are medications that you will more than likely have to take for the rest of your life."

In my mind, all I heard was Charlie Brown's teacher talking in my ear. I completely dismissed everything that he said because I, Johnnie Davis, had done extensive research online and I determined that these drugs were doing more harm than good in the long run. I asked, "Doc, are there any instances in which people have made full recoveries and did not require medication?"

"Yes," he responded. "There are documented cases but they are few and far between. Everyone is different and just because someone else was able to get off the medications doesn't mean that the next person will. Your heart condition is extremely serious, so you should just erase this notion of getting off your medications out of your mind completely." Well, quite naturally, this did not sit well with me at all, but what could I do? He was the doctor and I was the patient. I left his office with my tail between my legs because I felt defeated.

At some point in my mind, the doctor became my adversary instead of my advocate. I had to improve my heart function so I could show him that I wasn't like all of the other patients he had. I actually wanted to live and I didn't want to have to come and see him. I despised going to the doctor, hospitals, or anywhere else where sick people were. Just the very scent of a doctor's office or hospital gave me the willies. The less I saw him, the better off I was. I think I may have been the most defiant patient that he had.

I left his office, took the elevator down to the lobby, and walked back to my car. I sat there for several minutes pining over how I was going to get back to full strength. What could I possibly do that I hadn't already tried? I came up with my most brilliant idea yet! I drove home like Dale Earnhardt Jr. and jumped on my computer to find natural supplements that I could take to improve my ejection fraction once and for all. I spent hours on the computer just reading information on the heart and all of the minerals that it requires. I learned so much about Omega 3s, CoQ10, Krill Oil, Vitamins B6 and B12 just to name a few. I even studied the foods to eat and how much to exercise and which exercises to avoid. I studied it all! I was so determined to defeat this dreaded heart disease and live a normal life medication-free.

It's funny to think how when I asked my doctor about the vitamins and minerals, he knew very little of the benefits of them and nutrition in general. But he was well-schooled in the area of pharmacology. This proved to be yet again prophetic in a sense later on in my life. It didn't dawn on me at the time that he very well should have known about it nor did I ask why. I just looked at it as an opportunity to do something for myself instead of waiting around for something to happen. I went to the nearest health food store and purchased all of the vitamins and supplements that I researched earlier and I was extremely excited.

I thought I had found the solution to reverse this dreaded illness once and for all. I read so many testimonials on how the supplements helped people and, based on the description of their symptoms and diagnosis, we were similar. If it worked for those people, it would certainly work for me, I thought. Even though I didn't know any of them personally, I didn't have to. I had faith and that was enough for me. After purchasing all of the vitamins and supplements, I ran to the car and started taking them right on the spot. I didn't wait until the next day or anything. I just looked at the directions to see how many I should take with or without food, how many times a day, and boom! Down the hatch they went. Within hours, I began to feel better! That's what I told myself, at least. I thought to myself, *man, Johnnie Davis, you are on your way! The solution to your problem was at the health food store the whole time!* Are you kidding me? I couldn't wait to go back to see the doctor in a few months because I was sure my heart would have made significant improvements by then.

Several months passed, and it was time to go back to see my cardiologist. I was so excited to go this time because I hadn't missed one day of taking my new supplements and I was feeling amazing! I just knew my ejection fraction increased because I had more energy. My stamina and endurance had gotten better and so did my strength. I worked out consistently during that time and I was very pleased with my progress overall. I was like a kid that could not wait to show off his new toy for show and tell at school.

I arrived at the doctor's office and we started off with our usual conversation. "So, Mr. Davis, how you are feeling today?"

"Never better, doc, never better!"

"Really?" he said. "That's what I like to hear. Let's take your blood pressure... 120/80, very good! Okay, let's check your lungs. Take a deep breath for me. Ahh, sounds good. Have you been taking your meds regularly?"

"Yes, I have," I said.

"Excellent! What else have you been up to?" I told him that I added some vitamins to my daily regimen of medications such as

B6, B12, CoQ10, and Omega 3 Fish Oil. "Really?" he asked. "How has that made you feel?"

"Great so far. In fact, I feel better than great! If I were a dog with a tail, it would be wagging right now!" He burst out in laughter and told me how awesome that was. "Doc, when can we schedule another echocardiogram, so I can see where my ejection fraction is now? I mean, I feel absolutely amazing, so surely it has improved tremendously or else I wouldn't be feeling this way, right?"

"Well, we can certainly do it again, it's about that time. Let's schedule one for you within the next couple of weeks, how's that?"

"Sounds good to me, doc. Let's get the party started!"

After seeing the doctor, I took the order form to the front desk so the nurse could schedule my echocardiogram. I was beaming from ear to ear because I was just too excited. I thought that once he saw my awesome results, he would no doubt take me off the meds and I would just continue to take my vitamins and that would be it. I would much rather take something natural for the rest of my life than taking man-made toxic medications with God only knows what long-term effects.

The next two weeks seemed like two years! I can't recall a time before being more excited to have a medical procedure done in all of my life. I had to just stop and laugh at myself because the whole thing was funny to me. I always believed that there had to be a solution to my heart problem and that it was probably something very simple like taking more vitamins and such. I was going to prove them all wrong and defy conventional medicine. I would be the one that cracked this discovery wide open and would probably become famous as a result. Although that was not my objective at all, I just wanted to be cured and move on with my life. I thought that this could be the beginning of something special.

Two weeks went by and the day had arrived! This was the day I would celebrate my Independence Day from those prescription drugs, yes! It was Thursday morning and I wanted to be as early as possible so I could find out right away what my test would reveal. I got in my car at 7:30 a.m. and arrived at the doctor's office at 8 a.m. My echocardiogram was scheduled for 8:30 a.m. After signing in, I waited just a few minutes for my name to be called. When they called me, I popped up from my chair and was escorted to the back where the x-ray equipment and technician were. The tech was quite friendly and engaging, and she made me feel very comfortable. I laid down on the table as she stuck several electrodes to my chest. She turned on the echocardiogram machine and began to administer the examination. After about fifteen minutes on the table, I asked what the machine told her about my heart. I was anxious to know my ejection fraction. My heart was pounding because I couldn't wait to hear 55% or better. She looked at me with a smile and said, "I can't tell you that. You have to wait until the doctor tells you."

I smiled back at her and said, "Are you serious? You're the technician. Surely you can interpret what the data is telling you, right?"

"Oh, I most certainly can, but you see, I can't do that because I can lose my job. I'm not the doctor and only the doctor can do that."

"How long will it be before he gets the data and calls me with the results?"

"About a week or so."

"You have got to be joking! Do you know how long I've waited to hear the results?" I pleaded my case to her but she remained hellbent on her stance and refused to spill the beans. Finally, I said okay. I figured I had waited this long, I guess I could wait another week.

The following week, I received a phone call around noon on a Thursday. I answered the phone and it was the nurse from Dr. Shippman's office. "Good afternoon, Mr. Davis. I want to tell you that your echocardiogram results are in. Your heart did improve slightly and your ejection fraction is now 39%."

I said, "39%, is that all? Are you sure? I mean, I'm feeling great! My strength has increased and my stamina has…uh never mind. Thank you for the phone call. I really appreciate it."

At that point, I realized I was wasting my breath talking to her. Not only was she not interested in what I was saying, she couldn't help me. She just called to give me the results not to hear me rant about all that I had done to strengthen my heart and how I was feeling at the moment. Needless to say, I was quite disappointed because I expected to hear a higher number than that. But I finally came to my senses and said it did improve after all. I told myself it had only been a few months and a little improvement was better than none at all. *Don't be so hard on yourself. It's your heart, after all, not a sprained finger. Give it some time, you're on the right path.* After having this discussion with myself, I decided to take my advice and just celebrate the small victory and keep going. This was awesome. I was moving in the right direction and should be excited about it. Remain positive and, most of all, keep moving forward to where you desire to be. No one ever said it was going to be easy or fast. Some things just take time and there's no way around it.

Be patient.

It's important to engage in the right self-talk, especially when you're working toward achieving a specific goal.

CHAPTER 8

THE POWER OF FOCUS

From that day forward, I decided that I was going to live my life to the fullest. I mean a 39% ejection was low but I was still able to function. I was asymptomatic and my energy level was still high. I made up my mind that I was not going to be defined by that number. Most heart patients are obsessed with that number because it tells a lot about what's going on with your heart function. But it can also make you paranoid and scared to do anything because you're constantly thinking, should I do this or not? Is this bad for me? Will it make me tired? The doctor said don't do this, or go to this place, or don't get on a plane. I mean all kinds of stuff runs through your mind and can overwhelm you with fear if you feed into it.

I chose a different path. I chose to focus all of my energy on getting well and returning back to normal. I learned what the power of focus can do for you earlier in my business career. I conducted trainings on it and taught that what you focus on you become. It was time for me to activate this same principle and apply it to my own life. I didn't focus one day on being sick, having a weakened ejection fraction or anything that I did not want in my life. I only focused on getting well and getting stronger. I created a clear vision of me working out and lifting heavy weights without feeling lethargic. I envisioned doing wind sprints like I used to do in college and not get tired. I saw my heart shrink to normal size and my ejection fraction climb to 55% and higher.

I wrote all of these things out on paper and cut out pictures of athletes that I wanted to pattern my physique after. I needed to see the pictures every day in order to bury my vision deep into my subconscious mind. I understood the concept that thoughts are things and what you think about most is what you attract. So, if you say to yourself, "I don't want bills," you're going to get just that. Remember, life doesn't know how to take, it only gives what you put into it. So, a fundamental shift in thinking is required in order to make life work for you.

This is why I focused solely on getting well, and each step I took was a step in that direction with my workout regimen—taking my meds as prescribed regularly, proper nutrition, and exercise. I made sure that I did all that I could personally do to ensure that my health would be restored. I was not going to just leave my life in the hands of my doctors or any healthcare professional. I learned from my days of working in the health insurance industry that at the end of the day, you're a patient and a cpt4 code on a sheet that gets submitted to the insurance company so they can get reimbursed for their services rendered, period. No matter how nice of a guy I was, my doctor didn't love me like that. If I were to die, he would not be attending my funeral. So, yes, my life was up to me. I had to do my best to educate myself about all matters pertaining to the heart so that I could have more intelligent conversations with my doctor regarding my course of treatment and care.

The months were flying by and I felt pretty good for the most part. I was excited because this was an election year and our country was in dire need of change. My business had hit a wall and I was trying to figure out exactly what I was going to do next. The economy was in shambles and the real estate market was a bust. You could turn on every major news station and hear chants of "yes we can, yes we can." I became engrossed in this presidential race despite the fact that I absolutely despise politics. I think it's a complete charade and there is no difference between parties because they are both controlled by the same people. But this one caught my attention because, for the first time in history, there was an African American running for president and I thought, what a historical event this was. I never believed I would live to see such a thing happen, but there it was happening right in front of me, live in the flesh. It was an exciting time. People were ready for change in a big way. They wanted the Iraq war that President Bush got us into to end, gas prices to come down, and see jobs created and get people on their feet and back to work. It seemed like the perfect storm of opportunity for people to come together because it really didn't matter what race, color, or creed you were. Everyone was getting screwed and folks were sick and tired of it.

When the economy tanked and people were out of work, that was bad for my business as well. I was just getting back on my feet physically and I felt great about that. Now, I needed the government to do their part and get this country back on track. So, yes, I was extremely interested in this election because I wanted to see something done.

In the meantime, I was in dire need of reinventing myself, to come up with a plan that would allow me to bring more income into my household. I felt as if the walls were closing in on me. The bills began to attack me. I say "attack" because that's exactly what it felt like. I would pay one medical bill and two more would show up. I pay those two and three more arrived in the mail. It got to a point where I really just did not enjoy going to the mailbox anymore because I knew what was waiting on me. To the world outside, I was still Johnnie Davis, the man who kept it all together, who looked as if everything was excellent in my world despite my health challenge. But behind closed doors, I was living a life of quiet desperation.

Before moving from New Jersey in 2005, I had saved quite a bit of money from the business and I had plans to use that for investments, particularly in the real estate market to create another income stream. I had it all planned out. I was going to become a business mogul and have several streams of income coming in and I was going to enjoy early retirement and relax for the rest of my life. Maybe get married later on down the line, though I was in no rush to do that, so I was really looking at just enjoying my life as a healthy bachelor. Little did I know that I would get sick and the bottom would fall out from underneath me. I was completely unprepared for all of this and it cost me big time.

I learned a poem in college called the 12 Ps and it went like this. Piss poor preparation promotes piss poor performance. Piss poor performance promotes pain and the 13th P, was poverty. As I mentioned earlier, I had to pay for all of my medical expenses and I was still feeling the residual effects of that. There were so many bills coming in that I didn't know what to do. Physically, I felt fine, but, mentally, I was becoming depressed because I didn't know what I was going to do to get myself out of this financial rut. There was always a constant battle going on internally of trying to stay focused on improving my physical health and maintaining my sanity while dealing with strained finances. My mental stamina was running thin and I needed a boost in this area big time.

One day an idea hit me like a ton of bricks. The law of focus struck yet again. And in an instant I realized I needed to redirect my focus not on these bills, but how I was going to overcome this situation. I had to focus on the solution.

I went into my CD collection of personal development audio books and stumbled upon a disc that talked about asking the right questions. So, instead of asking myself, why do I have all of these bills, I should ask myself how can I eliminate them altogether? I put this principle into action and had a conversation with some former colleagues about restructuring and starting anew. All of us were kind of in a similar predicament because we worked very closely together and were financially tied to one another. We spoke every day on the subject of starting fresh and ridding ourselves of the dead weight of debt.

I contacted a gentleman that I knew was a financial advisor and gave him the rundown on my situation. He suggested that I restructure under Chapter Seven and start all over again. Now, I was extremely reticent to go this route because I heard so many negative things about filing for bankruptcy, like your credit will be shot to hell forever and you won't be able to do anything or get anything for years to come. Plus, it just seemed like the ultimate failure in life next to going through a divorce, which I had been through once already. I didn't know if I could emotionally handle it even though it seemed like the most viable solution at the time.

After several days of pondering my decision, I finally decided to go through the steps of proceeding with the restructuring process. I spoke with my financial advisor friend and he said to me, "Johnnie, it's not the end of the world. Powerful businessmen have filed bankruptcy many times. In fact, it's set up so that if you find yourself in this situation, as a business owner, you have the opportunity to start over. Do you know that Donald Trump filed bankruptcy at least three times? Look at him today; he's a billionaire. Johnnie, in the world of business, cash is king not credit. Don't worry about your credit. That will take care of itself in due time. However, focus on creating as much cash as you possibly can. Ultimately, that's what matters. If you have liquid cash on hand sitting in a bank, your credit will not matter as much."

After speaking with him, I felt so relieved and, in that moment, I realized another valuable lesson. It pays to have people skilled in areas of life that you're not, so you can get good advice from them. A wise man seeks good counsel before making a major decision.

He totally reframed how I was looking at the situation from being something negative to something positive, even strategic. It was a matter of understanding the system and how to make it work to your advantage.

A few days later, I called my attorney and he advised me on what steps to take to get the process started. I followed his instructions to the letter and in a matter of months, I was sitting in bankruptcy court. I will never forget the feeling of getting out of my car and walking toward the building. My heart began to pound profusely. I couldn't tell if I was nervous, embarrassed, scared as to who might see me, or if I was really having a panic attack. I think it may have been a combination of everything. This was only my second time going to court in my life, the first was to get a divorce. I was actually excited about getting a divorce from my first wife, but on this day, it was different.

I took a deep breath and told myself this was just like getting a divorce, except I'd be separating myself from debt I could no longer live with. When I put it in that perspective, it made sense and I was able to calm myself down and take the elevator upstairs to the third floor.

When the door opened, I stepped out and saw a mob scene of people there. I could not believe the amount of people also filing bankruptcy. These people were doctors, business owners, and other professionals that I didn't expect to see. Actually, I really didn't know what to expect because I had never gone through this process before. One by one the names were being called and I heard how this person's brand new BMW was part of the bankruptcy or that person's Mercedes S Class 550 and so it continued. People were giving up their homes and businesses because they just couldn't afford to keep them.

Many had lost their high salary jobs and the economy was extremely sluggish, so depending on what business you were in, you literally were not in business anymore. People were still reeling from the real estate crash from the year before. It was a myriad of scenarios as to why they were all there. I just remember not feeling so bad after all. I mean, I'm a self-employed business owner and I needed to restructure just like these fine people were doing. In my mind, that made everything okay.

My name was called and I sat next to my attorney. He told me ahead of time what questions they were going to ask and how to respond to each one. I did exactly as he instructed and, just like that, my financial troubles were over. All of my debt had been discharged! I looked at him and smiled. I got up, shook his hand, thanked him for helping me through this stretch, and I left the court room a happy man. All I could think about was if I had not asked myself the question of how I could eliminate this debt, this day may have never occurred. I walked out of the courthouse feeling ten feet tall and bulletproof with a new lease on life. I could recharge my business and get the cash flow coming back in and not be concerned with debt hanging over my head. Now I could devote every waking minute to getting as healthy as possible because things were finally looking up! I felt like so many other mega millionaires that had to restructure at some point in their lives.

Now that the restructuring was complete, I had to focus my attention on getting my business back on track. The financial burden of carrying too much debt had been lifted and now it was time to get back to where I was before I moved to Charlotte three years earlier.

I worked like a madman day and night. I was doing live meetings and traveling to conduct seminars all throughout the southeast. You name an event that was taking place and I was there. I really pushed my 39% ejection fraction to the limit. I flew back home to New Jersey to conduct meetings there as well as New York. It was nonstop. At the time, I was an executive in a company that sold legal and identity theft protection plans. If you're asking yourself what that is, think of the concept of legal insurance. You pay a small monthly fee to have access to a network of law firms across the US for any and all legal matters.

I began my corporate career in 1994, working in the health insurance industry and began working in the legal services industry part-time in 2001. It began as something to do on the side to earn some extra income. I was always interested in earning extra money doing something. As long as it was legal and didn't involve anyone getting hurt in any way, I was open to it. A friend of mine shared the concept with me and I understood it right away. I started with that company as an independent agent and went on to build a massive team throughout the northeast. Identity theft was really becoming popular and we had the best product on the market, so it was an easy sell.

After pounding the pavement for the next few months and traveling all over the eastern corridor, I was able to revive the team and get things moving in the right direction again. Money was flowing in and I could take a deep breath and relax. Although things were on the upswing in the back of my mind, I couldn't help but wonder how long it was going to last. Sure, I'm an optimist, but one thing my health challenge taught me was that nothing lasts forever. You have to roll with it and enjoy the moment while it lasts. Prepare as much as you can for the worst but don't focus on it. Create your own insurance policy for your life.

CHAPTER 9

UNDERSTANDING YOUR PURPOSE IN YOUR LIFE

Myles Munroe's book *In Pursuit of Purpose* is one that I hold near and dear to my heart. He said something that really stuck with me. "Without purpose, life is an experiment or haphazard journey that results in frustration, disappointment, and failure. Without purpose, life is subjective or it is a trial and error game that is ruled by environmental influences and circumstances of the moment. Likewise, in the absence of purpose, time has no meaning, energy has no reason, and life has no precision."

After reading that one paragraph, I figured out my problem. I had no idea what my purpose was for my life. I felt like my life was an experiment, a haphazard journey that resulted in frustration and failure just as he said. My health challenge and the restructuring of my business were perfect examples. I couldn't believe what I was reading. I asked God to show me the way and guide my steps in the direction that I needed to go in order to make a positive change in my life. He directed my steps right to my own library. The more I read the book, the deeper I understood what the meaning of my life was, and I started to feel a sense of clarity, one that I'd never experienced before.

Dr. Munroe also stated in his book, "No amount of accomplishments can replace the power of the motivation of finding your own special niche and working toward your dreams." I could not help but wonder how this man knew what was in my head. I was feeling this but just did not know how to articulate it.

I started thinking about what it was that I was doing from a professional standpoint. I was selling legal plans and identity theft protection services but I really was not excited about that. I was good at selling it and I was able to build and train a large sales team to go out and do the same thing and made a lot of money in the process, but was I really excited about it? I thought I was. The founder and CEO of the company's mission was to help people all across North America gain equal justice under the law. That's one heck of a mission because God knows there's a lot of injustice going on throughout the country. The mission was indeed noble and one that anyone could get excited about. But was that necessarily my purpose in life?

The job came with some nice perks but was that the only reason why I was doing this? I had to really ask myself some hard questions because I had built an entire business and career on this. If only I had come across this book beforehand, I may have decided to do something different, who knows. I had a hard time separating the fact that just because I was good at selling these services didn't mean that this was my life's purpose. I began to rationalize this by saying to myself, *Johnnie, you're helping people, right?* Look at all of the people in this country being railroaded by our legal system. We can offer something to help the little guy win. Truth is, I believed I was doing the right thing because it was a great service to provide. But I couldn't help but wonder if there was more that I could be doing with my life. How can I make more of an impact in the world?

If you ask empowering questions, you will receive empowering answers. I remember this exercise that I had learned from one of my wealth mentors years ago. It was the process of taking "self-inventory". I took out a sheet of paper and listed all of my strengths on the left side and all of my weaknesses on the other. The goal was to see all the things I did well and liked about myself, and work on either strengthening or eliminating the things I did not do well. As you can imagine, the challenge with doing self-exams like this is the honesty factor. It's a lot easier to ask someone to list these things about you, but the question is, can you honestly list these things about yourself without bias? Needless to say, that was tough. Nonetheless, I gave it a shot and began writing everything down.

When it came to the things I did not like or considered my weakness, I had to ask myself why these items were weaknesses and figure out a way to turn them into strengths, if possible. The list of strengths I came up with was training, coaching, leadership, motivating, and humor. My weaknesses were my health challenge, no clarity for my life, and no specific life plan. I had to stop there because I did not want to depress myself. I could work with the strengths because they were natural skills and talents, but my focus turned to my weaknesses because, based on what I read in Dr. Munroe's book, I believed the keys to my success were hidden there.

I began to study more and really delve into the world of personal development during this time. By no means was this my first rodeo with personal development but this situation was different. I needed to rewire my subconscious mind with positive affirmations with a clearer picture of my *vision* and also start to meditate. I heard of people doing it, especially successful professional athletes and business owners, but I never put much stock in it until now. I never understood how important it really was and all of the benefits it provided. I first had to learn how to do it, so I began researching how to meditate and the different forms of mediation.

Dr. Munroe describes meditation in this way and it just made complete sense to me. He said, "Imagine having a conversation with someone and you did all of the talking. After you were done, you just got up and walked away and did not hear the response of the person that you were talking with. You never received and answer to your questions or even heard that person's point of view or input. How effective was that?" He then went on to say, "Meditation is the practice of you sitting still and quieting your mind so that you can hear God's voice. The answers to your questions and your vision are revealed to you during this time of quiet and peacefulness."

All of I could think about were the times I prayed to God and it seemed that either he didn't hear me or I didn't hear his response, and I said to myself, now I know why. I gave him my list of demands, my troubles, my fears, my concerns, and then got up and just walked away without hearing the answers. All of this made so much sense to me. I began meditating and spending that quiet time with my thoughts and just clearing my mind of all of the noise and clutter of the outside world. I still wondered about the reason for my heart challenge in the first place. And the answer came to me in a dream.

I was sleeping one night and, for some reason, I smelled cigarette smoke in my room. Now, I knew it wasn't me because I've never smoked anything in my life and I loathe the smell of cigarettes. Besides, I was home alone and I was asleep! It appears that my father had come to visit me in my dream. My father passed away in 2003 and, unfortunately, we never had a chance to heal the old wounds that scarred me for life. I also never told him how I felt and how much I really needed him to be there in my life and how much I missed him growing up; or express the anger I felt and to just have that one good cry. He passed away before we had that father-son talk. Nevertheless, he appeared to me in a dream and he walked out of my room and into my living and sat on the couch. He then got up and walked through the kitchen out into the backyard. I noticed that the doorknob was broken as if someone had broken in. I looked at the doorknob and said to him, "Dad, why did you break in? You didn't have to break the lock to come inside; you could have just rang the doorbell."

He responded, "Don't worry about the doorknob, son, it's okay." I knew I was dreaming now because Johnnie Davis Sr. never called me son. I followed him out into the backyard and we went over to the side of the house where my bushes were and he said, "Son, you have to water your bushes. You have to water your bushes."

I said, "Okay, Dad, I will." And I followed him back into the house and he walked off into the darkness and disappeared. I didn't follow him there; I stayed behind and watched him fade away into oblivion.

That experience really shook me to the core because up until that point, I had never dreamed about my father. I didn't even cry at his funeral. I didn't understand why he appeared in my dream so vividly and that really freaked me out. I told my mother of the dream and she said he had come to visit her and my brother in their dreams as well. Now I was really afraid because I didn't understand all of this supernatural stuff. My mom and I talked some more about the meaning of the dream and the topic of forgiveness came up. She asked me if I had forgiven my father for everything he'd done in the past, if I had let go of the anger that I had been harboring all of those years since my childhood. She knew that I held on to a lot of pent up anger and resentment toward him my entire life. It never dawned on me that after all of those years, I had not let it go. I told her that I never did. The man was gone and had been for five years, yet for some reason, I just couldn't let go of the anger.

She said to me, "Johnnie, that's probably the reason why your heart went into failure. Do you know that harboring anger, bitterness, and un-forgiveness in your heart does more damage to you than the person you're angry with?" She was so right! My dad didn't know how mad I was and, quite honestly, didn't care. He was living his life and having a ball without care or concern for the family he left behind. And, yet, here I was holding this grudge against him all these years. I heard a saying that holding a grudge is like you swallowing a bucket of poison, hoping that the other person dies. It just doesn't work that way. The only person suffering is you and the other person has no clue of what's happening. I thought about that long and hard because all my life I had been masterful at holding grudges. If someone did something to me that I did not like or if I felt betrayed in any way, I would just disown them and felt really angry about it as if that was going to hurt them back.

I never liked being that way and I never knew exactly where that came from. I missed out on a lot of good friendships that I could have had over the years with some really good people. But I wasn't the best at forgiving. I just couldn't let go of the anger until I somehow got even. I had to return the same hurt and pain some-how, someway, and in most cases, I never did. My grudge was my grudge not my father's or anyone else's for that matter.

I was twenty-four hours away from expiring at the time I was diagnosed with idiopathic cardiomyopathy. This is where all the anger, bitterness, and resentment had gotten me. Wow, it was po-etic justice in a sense that God knew exactly what He was doing. The old Johnnie had to literally die in order for the new one to be born. My success wasn't going to come to me because I lacked intelligence, skill, and the drive to succeed. I needed a change of heart in the literal and metaphorical sense. I had to learn to forgive and let things go, especially things that were out of my con-trol. The bitterness, anger, and resentment I held on to led to low self-esteem, self-doubt, depression, unfulfillment, stress, and most of all, death. I believe I made myself sick and didn't realize it.

I'd been tested for everything under the sun and there was no definitive medical reason that caused my heart to malfunction.

Everything that I read going forward spoke of how maintaining a positive mindset, being happy, stress free, joyful, loving, and having a forgiving nature was good for the soul. All I could think about was how I was really kidding myself. No matter how many books I read or how many lectures I heard, seminars I attended or church services I went to, none of that could replace how I was really feeling in my heart. This is why meditation was so important for me to engage in because I realized I needed to rewire my hard drive and get all of that out of my subconscious mind.

The book of Proverbs 23:7 states, "As a man thinketh in his heart so is he." It doesn't say as a man thinketh so is he. I thought about becoming a millionaire and being healthy. I thought about living in my dream home and driving my dream car and having my dream wife. I thought about the quotes from all the books I had read over the years, but none of that mattered. All that mattered was what I had been harboring in my heart, deep in my subconscious mind. Dr. Munroe was spot-on with his assessment of how to tap into your success and discover your purpose. The key to my success lied in working on my weakness and the main one for me was learning how to forgive and love unconditionally.

You really have time to think about things when you're physically unable to run around like you used to. I suppose this was God's way of getting my attention. I'm not saying He had anything to do with my sickness—it appears that I may have brought that on myself—however, he had everything to do with the timing of me going to the hospital when I did and sending over an angel to take me to the hospital. Everything happened almost like clockwork and, for that, I'm eternally grateful. I was given another chance to get this thing called life right.

I was determined to become better at everything going forward. I committed to becoming a better son, brother, friend, business partner, leader, and ambassador for God by loving more and giving more of myself. I just had to figure out how to make things come together and create the life that I had envisioned for myself. I took out my notebook and began writing it all out. I learned from my personal development studies to write your goals down and make them as detailed as possible. The more vivid the description, the better, because it gives your mind something to work toward. Goals that are not written down are just wishes and we all know that wishes don't come true in most cases.

I began designing the life that I wanted to live and all of the things that I wanted to accomplish both professionally and personally, and that was my life guide. Each day I strived to do something that would take me a step closer to where I wanted to be in life. The first thing was getting my health back on track because without good health, you have nothing. I started going back to the gym regularly and working out. My ejection fraction at this point was hovering around 39% which was still low, but for me, I was functional and that's all that mattered.

I met with another personal trainer who helped me develop a routine that was heart-friendly. I also met with a nutritionist. Aside from taking my medication, proper diet and exercise was something that I could do to help myself. For my mental and emotional wellbeing, staying positive, meditation, prayer, and, of course, staying engaged in the personal development process was the key to maintaining a sound mind. I never had a problem with being disciplined to do something that was beneficial to me. I learned that principle early in life in catholic school. So, in my mind, this was the game plan and losing was not an option. I was ready to get the ball rolling and get my life back on track.

It was the spring of 2008 and I have to say that things got off to a phenomenal start. I felt like my health was improving because I was 100% asymptomatic. No swelling, no shortness of breath, no extreme fatigue, no brain fog, nothing out of the ordinary. Aside from the occasional sudden desire to take a nap, I was very functional and my mental health was awesome. I was consistent with my workout regimen and my business began to improve as well. My team was growing and my income increased month by month. Things were certainly headed in the right direction and I was excited about it. I developed a system that worked brilliantly for me.

There are four stages of consciousness that everyone experiences when they are going through a particular situation. We call this the cycle of development in business. The first stage is what we call unconsciously incompetent, meaning you are not aware of what you don't know. The second stage is unconsciously competent, meaning you are unaware that you know what to do. The third stage is consciously competent, meaning you are aware of what it is that you need to do to change a situation. The last stage is unconsciously competent, meaning you are on autopilot and you can do whatever needs to be done without thinking about it like brushing your teeth.

And it had all begun with Dr. Munroe's book. It completely transformed my thinking and made me realize that I was pursuing this thing called life all wrong. Prior to reaching this point, I had no plan, no clear long-term vision other than being successful in business, being happy, and getting married; all great things but extremely vague. I learned to crystallize my goals and write them out as detailed as possible with dates and timelines. I had to implement meditation and also state affirmations to myself every day. I had to rewire my subconscious mind and remove all of the gunk out of it and replace it with new beliefs and a new picture. I recited my affirmations day and night until I became unconsciously conscious and were a part of my essence. This process is something that doesn't happen overnight. It takes time and being consistent with doing these things daily.

My old thoughts and beliefs were developed over the course of three-plus decades, so it was going to take more than a few days, weeks, or months to accept a new identity. It all made so much sense when I wrote things out and thought things through. A major piece to the huge puzzle was to take personal responsibility for everything that happened to me in my life: good, bad, or indifferent. I was where I was simply because of me and not anyone else. I think it's human nature to look for someone or something else to blame when things don't go according to plan in your life. But it's much more liberating and empowering when you release that feeling of needing to place the blame outwardly and focus inwardly on how you can improve your life.

CHAPTER 10

IN SEARCH OF ME

My life was moving forward in the right direction but I couldn't help but feel that something was still missing. I discovered that, despite my efforts, I still didn't have a clear vision or purpose for life and it gnawed away at me. I learned the system of rewiring my subconscious mind by meditating and flooding it with new beliefs and a new life design, but I didn't have the actual road map to get there. What was the one thing that really got my juices flowing to live life to the fullest? What gave my life real meaning? Those answers still eluded me. I prayed and prayed and asked God to reveal to me what His purpose for my life was. I meditated on it and waited patiently to hear from Him. The response that I received was that I was supposed to help people change their lives. The only problem with that was, I didn't know in what capacity I was supposed to help them.

The last several years revolved around developing the leaders on my team. I shared the tools I had acquired over the years to help them blossom into successful entrepreneurs. And yet, despite that, I still felt there were other ways I could help people. But that was the one part of my picture that was still fuzzy to me. I concluded that perhaps this was the answer I was looking for and maybe I was overthinking the situation. Maybe I was supposed to help people gain access to the legal system.

Still, no matter what I told myself, I didn't feel fulfilled. But until I figured it out, I was going to keep reading the books, meditating, and attending the training sessions and seminars because I knew everything would work itself out. And you know what? It did, because not too long after that, my dearest friend, Rachel resurfaced and we were able to reconnect. We met in New Jersey at this swanky restaurant in New Brunswick back in 2003.

I will never forget the first time I saw her. She was with a group of friends and my eyes lit up like a kid on Christmas day. She was the most beautiful woman I had ever seen. Her fitted red dress was a nice touch, as I had never seen a dress fit someone quite like that before. We dated for a while before I relocated to North Carolina and then lost touch. She had moved from New Jersey and relocated to Georgia. She called me out of the blue one day just to check on me and see how I was doing. I really appreciated that. It was so nice to hear such a warm and friendly voice. We had a long conversation about what happened over the years and how we had fallen out of touch.

We never determined who was at fault for the long separation, but we both agreed it had been far too long and we wanted to do something about it. I lived in Charlotte and she lived in a suburb just outside of Atlanta, which was about three and a half hours away from me. I was never a fan of long distance relationships because I was of the mindset that they didn't work.

But I had reached a point in my life where I was going to live outside of my box for once. I told myself that life was too fragile and too short to live so rigidly. Little did I know, Rachel was making plans to relocate to Charlotte to take advantage of an opportunity that came her way. When she finally did, she wound up living ten minutes away from my house. She didn't tell me when or where she was moving. It just so happened that everything worked out naturally. I called it divine. As large as this city is, what were the chances of her moving within ten minutes of my house, knowing our history? It was meant to be and it wasn't long after she arrived to Charlotte that we began dating seriously and my life started coming together.

It was just as I had written in my Life Plan book. My business was on the upswing, my health was improving, and now my love life was heating up. Connecting with that special someone was really hard to do because everyone that was interested wasn't eligible. I had been in one failed marriage before and I wasn't about to make that mistake again.

At that time, I was young and didn't know anything about love or what a marriage meant. I got married for all the wrong reasons and that was simply because I had no idea what my life plan was. I was going along with society and what everyone else said I should do. This time it was a new ball game. I was older, wiser, and I'd been through some serious challenges throughout my life. I dated my fair share of ladies but no one stood out above anyone else. The only one that I could relate and connect to on an intellectual and emotional level was Rachel.

She was the complete package as they say. Brains, beauty, loving, caring and did not feel the need to compete with me. She showed me that she wanted to help me reach my goals and she was committed to doing just that. We traveled all over North Carolina and the southeast doing presentations, staying up late creating trainings, and not once did she ever complain or ask me for anything. She was always looking out for my best interest and what I needed. I had never experienced anything like that in my life and it was a major "aha" moment for me.

As great as things were going between Rachel and I, I was still grasping at straws, trying to get a handle on what the purpose for my life was. It was like a puppy dog following me around everywhere I went. I couldn't escape it. I went back to prayer and meditation, hoping to find something different, or at least, have something more definitive revealed to me; but I always came back to the same place. I turned to the one source that had been such a tremendous help in getting me this far and that was Dr. Munroe's book. I came across a passage that began to shed some light on the direction I was supposed to go. The passage read, "The world needs you and the purpose for which you were born. You also need the purposes of others in order to fulfill your purpose. Purpose cannot be filled in isolation." This spoke volumes to me because I understood it to mean that whatever I was going to do, involved others. I didn't know who, how many, or where they were but one thing was for sure, I couldn't do it alone.

This also made me think of exactly where I was in my business. I said to myself, I'm working with others and I'm not doing this alone. I must be at the right place, at the right time. According to what I read, this was pointing me back in that direction. But why was I still feeling so unfulfilled? That was the million-dollar question. I had no answer for that other than the fact that I was overthinking it again. *You're going to make yourself sick if you don't cool it and just roll with it. It will all work itself out,* I told myself.

So, in the beginning of 2009, I decided to roll with it and pursue the legal service business with a vengeance and really make some big things happen.

I locked in with my business partners at that time and we went to work. We traveled the country doing major event after event. We were helping new team members join our movement and helping others rise in the company. One of my favorite trainers, Zig Ziglar, says that if you help enough people get what they want, you can get what you want by default.

The emphasis has to be put on helping others succeed and that's exactly what we did. Team member after team member was getting promoted and lives were being changed right before our very eyes. I was so proud to witness people transform their bank accounts and grow into the leaders they desired to become. This made me feel absolutely amazing because I felt like I was making a contribution to the world and leaving behind a legacy in the form of successors. I imagine it's the same feeling parents have about their children when they see them do well and become productive citizens in society. All of the knowledge, wisdom, values, and training they imparted on their kids enabled them to make it in the world. That's exactly how I felt when someone called to thank me and tell me how much I impacted their lives. Or how much I inspired them to do more and become more; that was a feeling I couldn't explain. All I could think about was how this kid from the one of the worst housing projects in Newark, New Jersey was making a positive impact on the lives of so many people and the feeling was one of pure gratitude.

We attended our annual major company convention in Oklahoma City in the spring of 2009 and watched executive after executive walk across the stage. It was absolutely breathtaking to see everyone receive their awards and due recognition for their hard work and achievements. As a leader, it's what you live to see. It's one thing for you to create your own individual success, but it's another thing altogether to create successors because this is the true mark of great leadership. I started to look past what I did for a living and focus on the fact that I was investing and building people. When you build people, that's where the fortune is made.

As I sat in the audience with my partners, watching everyone walk the stage, everything that I read in Dr. Munroe's book made sense. It was all a matter of shifting my focus from making money to building people.

Now that my business was back on full throttle, it was time to direct my full attention to developing my relationship with Rachel. I learned one important thing after going through my rough patch and that was I needed balance in my life. All I focused on was me and the business because that's all I had. I was alive but I wasn't really living. I wanted to share my life with someone that loved me unconditionally. I thought about that a lot because I was getting older and did not want to miss out on true love. I know it may sound corny, but that was really important to me. I wanted to have children and not be the only person that I had to look out for. I had my business partners and the team but it wasn't the same. I knew a lot of single guys in the industry that were doing very well, earning multiple six and seven-figure incomes but they were still empty inside. At some point, the playboy lifestyle gets old and it was getting old for me in a big way.

My energy went to creating that balance in my life. Previously, it was filled with running around and building the business and that was fine because it was just me. I had no one to seriously consider other than myself. The thought of that made me feel very lonely at times. It's amazing how you can be surrounded by people all of the time, yet feel so alone. It seemed like the perfect time to put an end to this empty way of living and replace it with a more meaningful, loving relationship with someone special to me.

The following year in 2010, things were heating up with Rachel and I was really excited about where our relationship was heading. We often talked about marriage and having children, and I have to admit, those conversations were fun to have. Just imagining kids running around the house, playing with the dog in the backyard and taking family trips sounded really cool. The idea of going from playboy to husband to dad was cool but a little scary, too, because this was something completely different from what I was used to. I began to ask myself could I really do this? Could I be a good husband and father to our kid(s)? I thought about how my father left us hanging and how that made me feel growing up. How would I know what to do? I didn't have a great example to learn from. Unfortunately, there was no manual that I could read on how to be a great husband and father. So, after a while, I said to myself, *Johnnie you're doing it again. You're overthinking this. Just roll with it and learn as you go just as many before you have done.*

That Sunday morning, I went to church hoping to hear a good word that would further increase my confidence and provide me with a sense of clarity. I brought my notebook, ready to take copious notes as if I were going to a training seminar or something. The pastor began to teach not preach, and his message was spot on. It was as if he was talking only to me. He spoke about getting really clear on your goals and the things you wanted to accomplish in your life. He mentioned writing your goals down and making them plain. I said to myself, you have got to be kidding me! I've heard this before so many times, but this time, it resonated a lot deeper because this had nothing to with business. This had everything to do with my personal life. My level of awareness had been heightened because of where I was in my life.

I could have sworn the pastor had been reading my notes from a previous training I had conducted and was giving it back to me. I did exactly as he instructed the congregation to do. He gave us all a second to write down all of the things that we wanted to accomplish in 2010. Of the list of ten things I had written down, the main one was to find my bride. I wasn't even specific as to stating who my bride was going to be. He then said something that I will never forget and this was the thing that made me seal the deal. He spoke on the subject of marriage for a while because, after all, it seemed like all of the singles in the church were the subject of every sermon somehow. He said when it comes to making the commitment to get married, many men, in particular, shy away from it because they are overly consumed with thinking what it is that they are giving up versus what it is that they are gaining.

When he said that, it immediately struck a chord because that's exactly what I was doing. That's why I had shied away from the thought of marriage for so long. My focus was on the wrong thing. I thought about what I was giving up, the freedom of not having to answer to anyone, not having to find a babysitter, the visits to the in-laws, the compromising, and the other things that went along with being married. I never once focused on the fact that I was gaining a warm, loving, intelligent, strong, compassionate queen that would be an excellent mother to my kid(s), an awesome cook, and a strong business partner. I never once focused on the fact that I would be gaining a life partner and someone that would love me unconditionally forever.

When I shifted my focus and thought about those things instead of what I was giving up, there was no comparison. The proverbial light bulb went off and I knew what I had to do. It was easy for me make the decision because the love was already there. It was just a matter of getting my mind thinking correctly.

The crazy thing was after the pastor shared that part of his sermon with us, I literally didn't hear anything else. It was as if my brain just shut off because I had received exactly what I was looking for and there was no need to hear anything else. After the service ended, I left super excited because I had a game plan that I could implement right away.

Several days later, I visited Rachel at her apartment and we were having a friendly chat about the business and expanding into a new part of North Carolina. This part of the state was virgin territory for the business and I was excited about the possibility of pioneering an area and capturing a large share of the market. The more I talked about it, the more excited she became and she was extremely supportive. Her level of enthusiasm for my vision of what I wanted to do really excited me because I had never experienced this before with anyone.

I read in a book that the true definition of a friend is a person that is willing and committed and can help you reach your destiny. A friend is closer than a brother. I met a lot of people over the years that were willing, but not committed, to helping me reach my destiny. They were only interested in helping themselves reach their own destiny which is understandable. But to be committed to helping someone else reach theirs is the highest form of unselfishness and loyalty that you can find in a person, and that doesn't just come around every day. I knew that I had someone really special sitting right in front of me.

The plan was in motion and now it was time to execute it. We were going to expand our team into Rockingham, North Carolina because no one was out there doing the business. We had done our research before going to see if this would be worth our time, and based on the data we acquired, it appeared to be ripe for the picking. Rockingham was an easy two hours from my house, so we drove out there every Monday to see if we could start a local meeting in the area to kick things off. We were looking to identify key people that we could develop into leaders to take over the market. The first meeting was fairly successful. We had a decent turn out and several people joined our team that night. We went back the following Monday and a few more people joined and we thought we were picking up steam. We went back the following week, but this time, there were less people in the room and we were really disappointed because we were promised a packed house. We knew something like that could happen because that's how it was in the world of direct sales. We were just expecting to have better results because there was so much hype about the number of potential prospects coming to the meeting.

To drive all the way there and see less than half of the people in the room that were there the week before was exhausting. We drove out there for the fourth Monday straight, and this time, no one showed up. Can you say highly pissed off? What a waste of time! In an instant, all of my personal development went out of the window. I had to figure out what the problem was. How did we lose momentum so quickly? What had happened between week two and week three to cause such a dip in attendance? While I was busy trying to figure this out, there was one glaring fact that was staring me right in the face. Rachel was still there as supportive as ever, encouraging me to continue with the expansion and to not give up. I said to myself, what in the world? Where did you come from? Anyone else would have been screaming their head off, complaining, moaning, groaning, and whining about how much of a waste of time this expansion process turned out to be, but not her. She had my back 1000% and I could not ask for anything more than that.

On the ride home, we discussed if we were going to continue with the expansion into Rockingham and I told her that I would give it one more shot. I didn't want to keep going out there on empty promises. I needed to see more commitment from the new team members that were there. If they weren't going to commit, neither was I. I could certainly find something else to do with my time on a Monday night besides driving two hours away from home to go to a hotel conference room that I was paying for filled with excuses and no prospects.

Later that week, I had a call with the team and they all promised to fill the room. They were so apologetic for having us come all the way there for the past couple of weeks with such a low turnout.

The next Monday arrived and I went out there by myself this time. Rachel was unable to accompany me due to a prior engagement. When I got there, I noticed it happened yet again. The team showed up as promised but there were no guests taking a look at the opportunity. That night, I decided that the expansion project was over. Perhaps, we should have chosen a different city because this one was dry as a desert. I called Rachel and explained what happened. She told me not to worry about it and to try again next week. I told her there was no next week, that ship had sailed and I was done with Rockingham. We were going to have to target a new city with a new strategy. She quickly changed the subject.

"Have you eaten yet?"

"No, I haven't," I said. "Why, did you cook or something?"

"As a matter of fact, I did. Would you like to come over and have dinner with me?" I told her, sure!

After that, I think I sped all the way to her apartment. It was my lucky night because I knew I had broken some speed-limit laws driving through North Carolina. The boys weren't out and it was smooth sailing all the way. I'm almost positive I shaved off thirty-five minutes in travel time getting there. All I could think about was the food even though I didn't ask her what she had prepared.

I arrived at her apartment at approximately 9:30 p.m. and it smelled so good. I had no idea what it was but it certainly smelled scrumptious. Not to mention, I was starving so I'm sure that exacerbated it just a tad. I sat down in her dining area and she brought out sautéed shrimp, grilled salmon, and yellow rice with a glass of my favorite drink, cranberry juice. I was sitting in front of the plate with tears in my eyes because I was so hungry and the food looked delicious. I still couldn't figure out how she read my mind.

This was exactly what I was thinking about on the ride home even though she hadn't told me what she prepared. I knew we were meant to be. It was love at first bite. After devouring my meal, I thought to myself, *wow she can cook, too! Geez, man, what the hell are you waiting for, bro? Get off your butt and step to the plate before someone else does.* In that moment I like to call "the last supper", I asked her, "When is your lease in your apartment up?"

"In June, why?"

"What do you plan to do after that?"

"I'm thinking of buying a townhome. I need something bigger than this apartment."

"Don't do that. Don't waste your money. I have an idea. Why don't you let your lease run out, and when it's up, you can move in with me? I have a house and it's plenty big enough for the two us and then some. You don't have to leave your car outside anymore, you can park it in the garage. Also, what do you think about us getting married before the holidays?"

She stopped and stared at me for what seemed like an eternity. I think I may have caught her off guard just a bit with my offer. She went into the kitchen and poured herself a glass of wine. She took a huge gulp and then finally responded, "Are you serious? What brought this on? Was the food that good?"

I laughed out loud and said, "Well, as a matter of fact, it was and I can't stand the thought of you cooking like this for someone else. So, I'm suggesting that instead of you looking to purchase your townhome, move in with me and let's get married before the holidays. How does that sound?"

She just looked at me and stared. She took another sip of wine and smiled. I thought to myself, is she drunk already? Nah, can't be. She only had two sips. But she still didn't answer the question. Finally, she responded, "Yes, I will move in with you. Oh my God! Do you know how long I have been looking forward to this day? Wait a minute, this is not a joke, right? You're not going to have me move in and then change your mind or get brand new on me, are you? Johnnie Davis, don't play with my emotions like that. I'm a Haitian woman and we don't play like that!"

I looked at her and smiled then said, "Yes, I'm very serious, and, no, I'm not going to change my mind or get brand new on you. I want to be with you and I want you to be my wife."

She screamed and happily said, "Yes, yes, yes!" This turned out to be much easier than I thought. I wasn't nervous at all. I remembered what the pastor said in church a month or so earlier. Once I changed my focus from what I was giving up to all of the things I was gaining in a marriage. It was a no-brainer!

I would have been the world's biggest idiot for not sealing the deal with Rachel. She showed me all that I needed to see and I wanted us to get married the same year, right before the holidays. I really didn't see the need for a long-term engagement because we knew each other for so long. Even during our on and off periods, we always kept in touch and we developed a deep respect, admiration, and love for one another. It was the love that transcended everything, especially during the times when we did not communicate as much. It never died. So, to me, that's how I knew it was real. That early Sunday morning, sitting in church, hearing that sermon, was the catalyst to making it all happen. I wrote down on paper that I wanted to find my bride and I did. There's something magical about writing your dreams and goals down. It makes it official. Unwritten goals are just dreams that never come true.

CHAPTER 11
LOVE AND MARRIAGE

The big day finally arrived and my stomach was doing back-flips. I could not believe I was about to go through with this again, and for the last time. I was both anxious and excited. We decided to have a simple ceremony at the courthouse because we were both married before and each had the big wedding experience. We just didn't see the need in doing that again. It was all about the marriage, not the wedding. We both learned that lesson much later in life. We asked two of our good friends to be witnesses at our ceremony along with Rachel's mother and younger brother. They drove up from Georgia to join us and we were happy to have them. My family was in New Jersey at the time and my mother and siblings were not able to attend, unfortunately.

Everyone was at our house, waiting for us as Rachel and I got dressed. Rachel's friend, Angelica, was sitting in the living room, watching something on TV and I had come out of the bedroom trying to fasten my pants. Apparently, I had put on a few extra pounds unbeknownst to me because I was having the most diffi-cult time fastening the button on my waist. I was so embarrassed because I really didn't know where those extra pounds had come from. They snuck up on me like an old unpaid bill.

My tailored dress shirt was extra tight, my suit jacket was tight, everything was tight! I couldn't believe I was having wardrobe issues on my wedding day. I never thought about getting fitted for anything because my clothes always fit like a glove. But something happened between the time I got my clothes made and this day that I somehow missed.

I stood in the corridor of my bedroom and living room, talking to Angelica about something on TV, and trying to fasten my button at the same time. I sucked in my stomach one last time, and, finally, I was able to button my pants. As soon as I let my stomach out, the pressure must have built up or something because the button suddenly popped off, flew across the room, and struck Angelica smack in the middle of her forehead and onto the floor.

She erupted in laughter and so did I. I couldn't believe what just happened. I, Johnnie Davis, Mr. Physically Fit, was too fat for his pants and I turned them into a weapon. Rachel came running out of the bathroom, asking what was so funny. Angelica explained that my button flew off my pants, across the room, and hit her in the forehead as tears ran down her face from laughing so hard. Rachel began laughing, too, and, soon, her mom and brother came downstairs and joined in on the hysteria. I was so embarrassed. I felt like Carrie in the movie *Carrie* when the pig's blood fell on her and everyone in the gymnasium was laughing at her. All I kept hearing in my head was, "They're all going to laugh at you."

After standing there looking stupid, I laughed, too. Hell, it was funny. I couldn't believe it. That had never happened to me before, ever in life. What a way to kick off the day! We were running short on time and we had to leave so we could be at the courthouse by 1 p.m. and it was almost noon. Needless to say, I didn't have enough time to sew the button back on, so I wore those pants clipped on at the waist with no button and a belt to cover it up.

We hopped in the car and drove to the courthouse together. Angelica drove her own car and our other friend met us there. During the ride to the courthouse, her mother was certain to inform me that although she was getting married today and was going to be my wife, that I must remember that I have to share her with the family, too. I burst out laughing because I knew exactly what she meant. Rachel and her mom were just as close as me and my mother were, so I understood. I told her, "Mom, don't worry. I promise I will not infringe on your mommy-daughter time." I had no problem with that. I was thinking, *more time for me in the man cave, gotta love that!*

We arrived and stood before the judge as he read us our rights, I mean vows. We both said, "I do," and just like that, we were Mr. and Mrs. Johnnie Davis! It was the happiest day of my life. It was also the easiest thing I had ever done. Marrying Rachel was like putting my hand into a glove. It was a perfect fit and at the moment we exchanged vows, I had only one regret. I regretted the fact that I hadn't done it sooner. I knew from this day forward that my life was going to be changed forever and I was looking forward to our new adventure as a unit. My attitude was one of, watch out world, the Davis' are coming and we aren't taking any prisoners.

Later that day, we went to this exclusive restaurant to celebrate our nuptials with our wedding party and it was incredible. We didn't have a traditional reception filled with hundreds of people, music, and dancing. We kept it really simple and intimate. We had an amazing dinner with our family and the conversation was great. We were all so excited and just living in the moment of joy and happiness. It was the perfect ending to a magnificent day.

Soon after we were married, we attended our first event in Charlotte as husband and wife, but no one knew we'd gotten married. In fact, the only people we told were our immediate family members and a few close friends, but that was it. We just didn't feel the need to announce it to the world, so we figured we would just let people find out on their own. We arrived at the event and listened to the guest speaker. After he finished his presentation, he invited all of the leaders to share their testimonial as we customarily did at all of our company events.

We shared ours, but this time it was different. I spoke first and said, "Hi, we are Johnnie and Rachel Davis," and before I could finish, the room erupted with cheers and congratulations. Some people started crying and came up to give us hugs and handshakes. It was overwhelming. I didn't realize how happy people would be for us. After all of the fanfare, I finished our testimonial and we sat down in our seats. The room was still buzzing from the announcement throughout the rest of the training, and I have to admit, it felt good to be respected and loved in that manner from people that you've been building with for so long. After the event was over, we left the room and went out into the hallway area and everyone, I mean everyone, stopped us to congratulate us and give us their blessings. We felt like celebrities! We finally left the hotel and walked back to the car and still couldn't believe the reception we received. I imagine it would have been like that if we had done it the traditional way and invited all of those people in the room to attend. But, nonetheless, it was still an amazing feeling.

The plan was coming together just like I envisioned it would. We got married on November 12th and made it just in time to celebrate our first Thanksgiving and Christmas holidays together as a family. We were no longer the boyfriend or girlfriend that family members spoke about behind your back because they were trying to figure out who you were and didn't know if you would be around next year. I had been there and done that before and I hated being that guy.

New Year's Day of 2011 arrived and we were fired up about the future. Rachel and I wrote our goals down for the year and all of the things we wanted to accomplish. First thing was to take the business up another ten notches so we could save some money to purchase a bigger home in a different part of town. We wanted to set things up for our children. We also wanted to clear any lingering debts that we both had. Luckily for me, I had taken care of that already so I could help her eliminate hers.

We hit the ground running and were building like crazy. Our team exploded and the income from the business spiked! Things were amazing. I felt awesome for the first time in a long time. I made a commitment to slim down and drop a few pounds because I remembered how tight my pants were on our wedding day. Prior to that day, I had never had an issue with weight. I chucked it up to all of those late-night meetings with our team that ended at some restaurant where I was eating the wrong foods late at night.

Despite the challenges, I made a commitment to change my eating habits and to do more cardio exercise to drop a good fifteen pounds. Over the course of the following month, that's exactly what I did and I felt incredible!

One day I had set up a meeting with one of the market leaders in the area to discuss business and I noticed that he wasn't in the best shape. I didn't say anything to him right then but I made a mental note of it. Later that evening, we had our weekly business overview and I scanned the room as I stood on stage and I couldn't help but notice how out of shape so many people were. Not only were the guests looking out of shape, but the team members looked unhealthy, too. I never paid any attention to this before, but for some reason, it was sticking out like a sore thumb.

My reticular activation system also known as RAS was kicking in. You ever purchase a car and then all of sudden notice that everyone has your same car or at least it appears to be that way? That's your RAS kicking in. Now that you have that particular car, your awareness is heightened so you start noticing it all the time. The cars just didn't appear out of nowhere, they've always been there. You just hadn't noticed. That's the same thing I was experiencing in that moment of me scanning the room. The more

I exercised and lost the excess weight, the more I noticed how unhealthy people really appeared to be. It was a mind-blowing trip to say the least because it was as if someone pulled the wool from over my eyes and I was able to see clearly for the first time.

This really impacted me because now I was a married man with someone to think of beside myself. I needed to be as healthy as I could be, not just for me, but for my wife and our future kids. This was not only going to be the year that we took our business to the next level but I was also going to get into the best physical shape of my life. The thought of me becoming sick and being a burden on my wife was something I couldn't bear to imagine. I had been through that experience before and I couldn't imagine going through that again because she didn't deserve that. She deserved the best Johnnie Davis I could produce and I was committed to being that.

So, 2011 was the year of getting back to my old self and then some. Never again would I be in a situation where my pants didn't fit because I was too big. At five-foot-ten inches tall, I had no need to be 218 pounds. That was my heaviest and I didn't like the way I felt on my wedding day. Although it was the happiest day of my life, I didn't necessarily feel that great. Sure, I laughed it off when the button flew off my pants, but I was not laughing on the inside. I used that feeling as motivation to help me drop those extra fifteen pounds. Now you may be saying fifteen pounds? That's it? Talk to me when you have an extra fifty to 100 pounds to lose. An extra fifteen pounds on me with a weakened heart muscle was a big deal. I didn't need extra fat on my body to cause my heart to work any harder than it had to.

Summer came and I was slimmer and feeling fantastic. Each time I went to the see my cardiologist, the report was excellent, and it appeared that my heart was finally stabilized. I asked time and time again about the possibility of me coming off the medications because I knew how bad they were for me.

I wasn't focusing on how I was feeling at the time. I was looking down the road and how other parts of my body could be affected over time. This was the extremely frustrating part to discuss with my doctor because he would always give me the same answer. He would say, "Mr. Davis, unfortunately, I don't know what to tell you regarding the long-term side effects of the medications you are taking. These drugs are fairly new and there is just not enough clinical data to show what the long-term effects. Are there certain risks with taking any medication? Yes, there are. But I can't tell you how they are going to affect you years from now. Who knows with modern medicine? There are breakthroughs occurring daily and there may come a time where you don't have to be on your medication. But as far as you coming off now, I don't see that happening. However, if your heart shows improvement and your ejection fraction increases to the normal range and stays there, I don't see why we couldn't at least have the discussion."

It wasn't quite what I wanted to hear but at least there was hope. I figured if I could somehow get my heart to improve its function, I would live longer and all would be right with the world. So, I turned my attention back to improving my health and continuing to build our business. I was determined to live as long as possible and I didn't want to ever look like the audience I had seen at the meeting.

I coasted along during the fall and winter of 2011, still enjoying the fact that I was a husband and I was feeling great. My attitude was positive and all was awesome in the Davis household. I was really living the dream. We celebrated the holidays with our family and we couldn't have been happier. I was thirty-nine years old, looking forward to turning the big 4-0. There was a time when I didn't know if I would make it there based on what I was told, but I never let that bad news weigh me down. Not only was I going to make it to forty but I was going to step into the "Over 40 Club" like a boss! Nothing was going to stand in my way. I have to admit, in the back of my mind I was a little scared because I really didn't know what to expect.

All of those disheartening conversations I had early on about my heart issue still lingered in my head. This is why it's so important not let certain things enter into your subconscious because it records everything whether you know it or not. I was there and I heard what the doctors said about my long-term prognosis and I did my best to dismiss anything I did not agree with. But my subconscious heard it as well, recorded it, and stashed it away in my mental file cabinet only to pull it out when I was on my way to achieving a new goal or milestone in my life. I guess this is how some people self-sabotage themselves. They choose to focus on the negative picture instead of creating a positive outcome. This, in turn, prevents them from blossoming and achieving whatever dreams they may have. I chose to ignore the fear and feelings of apprehension and proceed to forty anyway.

I welcomed forty with open arms and I was going to have the biggest birthday celebration to bring it in. I made my decision years ago to get busy living and not focus on dying. However, I have to admit that thought did cross my mind every now and again and it was a challenge in making it stop.

January 6th arrived and I made it to forty! I went to the bathroom and shed a tear of joy because I made it. God spared my life so that I could see this day and enjoy it with all of my friends and family. I was feeling great and I was ready to get the party started! My siblings had arrived the night before and stayed at our house. The day flew by pretty quickly with making last-minute preparations for this mega event, not to mention the pure excitement of it all. We drove down to the club together later that night to get the party going.

Once I arrived, the party officially started! The music was awesome and the food was incredible. I couldn't remember the last time I partied like that. It must have been in college or something.

I hadn't danced like that in years. I mean when I was done danc-ing, my shirt was drenched with sweat. Now this was completely uncharacteristic of me because I'm not the one that would party to the point of being drenched. I'm more conservative and cool in a party atmosphere. But this night, I said what the hell. I only turned forty once and I was going to live it up because tomorrow is not promised. So, if I look stupid, I don't care. It's my birthday! I'm going to live in the moment and appreciate every second of it and that's exactly what I did.

The party was insane! I had the best time ever. My wife really outdid herself with the preparations, food, DJ, cake and making sure all of my friends and family made it to Charlotte. It was the best 40th birthday gift ever. But the party didn't stop there; she ac-tually booked a trip to the Dominican Republic at a luxury resort in Punta Cana. I was overjoyed when she casually told me to pack my bags. At first I thought she was joking but when I discovered she wasn't, I think I ran through the house singing something in Spanish and I don't even know Spanish. I don't know what in the world I was singing but it sounded good to me. I had never been to the Dominican Republic and I looking forward to getting away from the bitter cold to someplace nice and warm, sipping on drinks I couldn't pronounce. Turning forty was the best thing I could have ever done!

My party was on a Saturday night and we flew from Charlotte to the Dominican Republic on the following Monday. It was unusu-ally cold on this day and we were bundled up. I couldn't help but wonder if we were just a little over dressed since we were headed someplace where the temperature was a warm eighty-five degrees in January. When we arrived in the Dominican Republic and got off the plane, the heat sucker punched me in the face like Mike Tyson.

I had on a thick sweat suit and a leather coat and I felt like I was walking through an oven. I couldn't wait to get to the resort to take all of that stuff off. I was ready to eat, sit by the pool or on the beach, and just do nothing. We went through the security gate and made it to the shuttle that was going to take us to our resort. We got on the shuttle and the driver was very friendly, playing bachata music over the loud speakers. It made the ride fun and festive all the way there. I thanked Rachel on the way to the resort, because until this point, I didn't realize that it had been a few years since I had taken a real vacation. I was so focused on getting my health and business back on track that I never even thought about going on vacation. But that was exactly what I needed!

We arrived at the most beautiful picturesque resort I had ever seen and I felt like I was in paradise. We got off the bus and walked to the check-in area of the resort and it looked like a slice of heaven. The flowers, bushes, architecture and landscaping were just magnificent. I didn't want to leave this place ever!

We checked in and got our room keys and caught a ride to our room on the golf buggy. When we got there, we both changed our clothes immediately and went straight to the beach. The Dominican people were very warm and friendly. I really felt like I was at home. The only thing was I couldn't speak the language. People greeted us with hugs and really big smiles and I was a little taken aback by the response at first because it was as if they were treating us like celebrities or something. I wondered if they were trained to treat the tourists this way or if they thought Rachel and I were famous? Anyway, it didn't matter because I loved the treatment regardless. We met people from all over the world vacationing from Canada, England, France, Russia, and some of the coldest places on earth during the winter months. They were referred to as snowbirds by the islanders.

All of the people we met were incredibly friendly as well. I had a really great conversation with this lady from England. We talked about everything from religion, politics, current world events to the conspiratorial view of history. I found it fascinating how much we had in common on a lot of these issues and it was mentally stimulating. At the end of the conversation, she said, "It was really nice chatting with you, Eddie."

I said, "Eddie? Who's Eddie?"

She said, "Why you are, my dear. Aren't you Eddie Murphy?" I burst out in intense laughter! All this time, she thought she was talking to Eddie Murphy.

I looked at Rachel and I said to her, "Wow, who knew?" I laughed again then finally told her, "No, I'm not Eddie Murphy. I'm Johnnie Davis from North Carolina." She turned beet red with embarrassment.

"I'm so sorry," she said. "You look just like him."

"Eddie has hair, I don't. It's okay. I get that all the time."

We laughed about this the entire day and night. The trip was getting off to a fantastic start it was only day one of a seven-day trip and already I had been mistaken for a celebrity. I was curious to see just how far this would go.

As time went on, we continued to receive the red-carpet treatment everywhere we went. Every restaurant that we dined in, the chef would personally come to our table to greet us. We were given extra food and drinks and never waited in line for anything. I said to Rachel, "Now this is the life." I loved this preferred treatment and could get used to it very quickly. Many of the employees were of Haitian decent since Haiti and the Dominican Republic share the same island only separated by a border. Since Rachel is Haitian she spoke fluent Creole. When the employees found out that she was Haitian and spoke the language, it was a done deal. Everyone on the resort knew exactly who we were and we were treated like rock stars! This red-carpet VIP treatment sure did spoil me because I couldn't walk anywhere on the beach/resort without someone calling me or trying to get my attention somehow.

It turned out that the workers weren't used to seeing people that looked like them and one that spoke their language on vacation during this time of the year with all of the snowbirds. I was completely astonished by this because, as I looked around the resort, I saw why we stood out like sore thumbs. We were the only people of color that were not employees. Not to mention, they, too, thought I was one famous athlete or another. Whenever someone called me by some athlete's name, I just went with it and I had a blast! If it meant getting extra shrimp with my meals or beverages for Rachel, I was whoever they thought I was. We had the time of our lives.

CHAPTER 13

BACK TO BUSINESS

The week in paradise flew by so fast and it was time go back home to cold, wintry North Carolina. Although I thoroughly enjoyed myself on vacation, I was a little anxious to return home and get back to work. Rachel and I set our goals for the year and we were ready to get back and execute the game plan. We both decided that we loved going on vacation in January while most people were just recovering from holiday shopping. We wanted to keep this up and actually take even more vacations during the year. But in order to do that, we had to get to work and take our business and team to the next level.

We returned home and jumped right back into the fire and hit the ground running with building our business. We conducted business overviews, weekly webinars, home meetings, you name it. We turned up our personal activity and the business was booming.

By early Spring, our company had come out with a new car bonus program and I had qualified for it. I also received another award for enrolling over 1000 personal customers which was a huge accomplishment. I went and picked up my new 7 Series BMW and at the next convention I walked across the big stage to pick up my 1000 Application Award. Life was moving in the right direction.

Health-wise, I was feeling stronger than ever and I was extremely optimistic about our future. Our goal was to continue working our business and saving our money so we could move into our dream home and start a family. Everything was going along so smoothly.

In the fall of 2012, I went to see a new cardiologist for a routine visit and we talked about my heart function. He was just as baffled as I was regarding my diagnosis and suggested I undergo some tests to see if they could actually find a cause. I was more than excited to comply because I wanted to know, too. I could never accept the fact that there was no known cause for my idiopathic cardiomyopathy. It took me years to even admit that cardiomyopathy was the same as heart disease. I jumped at the opportunity to find out what was happening.

I did a heart catheterization and the results came back normal. There were no blockages in my arteries at all. In fact, the doctor said that my arteries were so clear that everyone should have clear arteries like mine. I did a stress test and the results from that were good as well.

Meanwhile, I was still exercising on my own and feeling pretty good for the most part. Rachel decided that she wanted to join me in getting healthy because someone posted a photo of her on FB that she didn't like. She had on a beautiful red dress and it was taken at our last convention. Now, when you're newlyweds, one of the most noticeable things that tends to happen is that both people gain a few extra pounds. I was okay because I worked out regularly, but Rachel on the other hand, did not. She had put on a few extra pounds during our two-year marriage and, apparently, didn't notice until her friend posted that picture of her on social media.

Rachel called her friend and told her to remove the picture immediately because she did not like the way she looked. She then asked why I didn't tell her that she'd gained some weight.

"You gained weight?" I asked. "Where? I don't see it."

"Yes," she said. "I gained an additional thirty pounds of happy weight and I'm no longer happy with it!" I saw it but I knew better than to tell her that. I love to sleep peacefully at night.

We hired a personal trainer and he created a regimen for her to follow for the next thirty days. They worked out religiously and I was so proud of her because she really did not enjoy exercising but she was dedicated to the process. She was determined to shed those extra pounds. Thirty days went by and, although she had committed to all of the training sessions, she saw very little results. In fact, she hadn't lost an inch or pound and we thought that was really odd.

They had a discussion about her nutrition and what she was eating after they completed the sessions. Turns out, there were some major changes that needed to be made with her diet, so he introduced her to a nutritional cleansing company called Isagenix. Neither one of us had ever heard of the company before. She started the program and achieved some unbelievable results with the system. I was so excited for her because she was able to achieve in thirty days using this program what she couldn't accomplish just working out with the trainer and trying to stick to a "clean diet".

I had no interest in the program because I thought I knew all that I needed to know about exercise and nutrition, so I never even gave it a second thought. I was happy with where I was physically and didn't need to try a weight loss program.

The following month, I went back to see my cardiologist to get my echocardiogram results. I was so excited about this visit because I was expecting to hear some great news. I went to the gym earlier that morning before going to see the doctor and had the best workout ever! I was feeling super strong and my stamina was amazing. I worked with free weights for an hour or so then finished my routine with thirty-five minutes on the treadmill. I wasn't tired or short of breath. I didn't feel any chest pain or dizziness. In

fact, I felt like I never had a heart condition at al
say, I was pumped about hearing what the doctor

Rachel and I arrived at his office later that aft
mally when the doctor saw me, he greeted me wi
firm handshake. This time, he wore a different expression on his
face. It was one of deep concern and worry. We walked into his
office, sat in the chairs across from him, and then he lowered the
boom on us.

"Johnnie, I'm sorry to say that the results from your echocardiogram were not what we were expecting at all. Your ejection
fraction has decreased from 39% to 25% and you need to have
a defibrillator implanted in your chest today because you can go
into sudden cardiac arrest at any time."

Now, Dr. Jones and I had this conversation before but it was just
a worst-case scenario conversation that neither one of us thought
we would have to seriously consider because I was progressing
steadily. I was in complete shock when he said this and it took all
of the wind out of my sails. I had done all that I could do within
my power to help strengthen my heart and it still wasn't enough.

Despite needing the defibrillator implanted in my chest immediately, my insurance would not pay for it because I was only forty
years old and asymptomatic. He said that I could appeal their
initial denial, but by the time they review the medical records and
respond back, I could very well experience sudden cardiac arrest.
I asked how much it would cost and he said it was about the same
amount as a luxury vehicle and that was just for the device. That
did not include the hospital stay, anesthesia, lab work, etc.

"You're looking at well over six figures to have this procedure
done."

Rachel and I looked at each other in shock because we didn't
have an extra $150,000 lying around in our bank account for sur-
gery when we both had health insurance to cover it. "What are my
options?" I asked him.

"You don't have any," he said. "If you don't have this device implanted in your chest right away, there's going to be a tragedy in your household and I don't want to see this happen to you and your family." I looked at Rachel and her mouth dropped to the floor. She had this look on her face like she was going to break down and cry. I forgot about what the doctor said in that instant because all I wanted to do was take Rachel's pain away.

I had several emotions rush through my body at once. I was angry, sad, anxious, scared, tired, frustrated, and confused all at the same time. *What the hell am I going to do now?*

"Doc, how is this possible? I mean, I take my medications as prescribed, stick to a healthy diet for the most part, and I exercise regularly as recommended. I feel great most of the time. In fact, I just left the gym prior to coming here today. How can I feel great but be sick at the same time?"

"That's the thing with cardiomyopathy. You can be feeling great some days and feel like crap others. Because you work out so much and you don't abuse your body with alcohol, bad foods, drugs or cigarettes, you're feeling great. But your body is functioning on fumes and eventually your heart is going to give out on you. I don't want to see this happen to you. I've been a cardiologist for fifteen years now and I've seen this happen time and time again. I'm being as upfront with you as I possibly can be. The choice is ultimately yours in terms of how you want to proceed, but you have all of the information in front of you to make your decision."

For some reason, I was deathly afraid to have this ICD implanted in my chest. The mere thought of having a metal device wired to my heart scared the shit out of me. I consulted with several colleagues on my team that were physicians and I explained to them what my situation was. They all assured me that it was no big deal. It was a common, simple procedure that a lot of people had every day. They all told me I'd be fine and not to about it. But it was easy for them to say because they didn't have to have the device implanted in them. People are always quick to give you advice that they themselves would not take.

Because I was so afraid to have the procedure done, I decided to get a second opinion from another cardiologist to see if there was a new drug or some type of new therapy treatment that I could do to help me. I was willing to try anything but have heart surgery. Besides, there was the little problem of not having $150,000 lying around in the heart surgery fund that put a huge damper on things. I was mad at myself because I didn't have the money. As hard as I worked, and as large as my team was, I should have had it. This was another huge lesson to learn from. People say money can't buy you love and it won't make you happy. It may not be able to do those things but it can sure save your life when you need it to. I'd rather have more than enough of it and not need it than to need it and not have it.

After I finally calmed down and got over the fact that all that I had done to preserve my heart and health was all for naught, I decided to get the second opinion anyway. In the back of my mind, I kept hearing Dr. Jones say, *you don't have any other options. You need this device, you need this device.* It was echoing in my head over and over again. I called my original cardiologist and scheduled an appointment. I met with him three days later and we discussed my situation along with changing my medications. He told me that the medication I was on was a really low dosage, a baby dosage, in fact.

Really? I had been taking a baby dosage of medication for two or so years. Could this be the reason why my heart didn't improve as much as anticipated? He said that it was quite possible. I asked why I was still asymptomatic and he told me that he didn't know the answer to that. The disease could be very tricky for some. Other than my heart, I was in excellent health.

If I were battling diabetes, obesity, or, perhaps, was a smoker, I might have experienced symptoms and my outcome may have been very different. He suggested we increase my dosage to the maximum to see if that would help improve my heart function over the course of the next three months. If there was still no improvement with my ejection fraction, then he highly recommended I get the defibrillator. I agreed to do it, but there was still one problem. If it didn't work, where would we get the $150,000 for the surgery?

I walked out of his office with the hope that all was not lost. There was still a chance that this could turn around. I was determined to keep fighting the good fight and give it my 100% focus. I took my new prescription straight to the pharmacist happier than a kid in a candy store because I was looking at it as not only the wonder drug, but my last resort to strengthen my heart. In addition to praying daily, asking God to heal my heart, I had nothing or no one else to turn to for help.

Two weeks went by since I got the new prescription, and so far, so good. Thanksgiving was coming up and everything seemed to be going well. I really couldn't tell if I was experiencing any improvement because I always felt great. I was going on blind faith that the medication was doing what it was designed to do and that all would work itself out.

I made it past Thanksgiving and, boy, was I extremely thankful to see another one. I went to sleep every night knowing that my ejection fraction was 25% based on what Dr. Jones had said just two weeks prior. He told me I could be driving my car and just pass out at a red light. I could fall asleep and go into sudden cardiac arrest and not wake up and I wouldn't feel a thing. I did my very best to block that out, but it was always on my mind. I had to try and stay positive not just for myself, but for Rachel, too. I didn't want her to live in fear of knowing something fatal could happen to me and she couldn't do anything about it.

December 2012 ushered in and Rachel and I were both looking forward to this one because we were also in the process of planning our family. We had gone through all of the necessary steps to begin the invitro fertilization process and everything was looking awesome. We were expecting her to get pregnant in January and have the baby born in September of 2013. That's all I thought about twenty-four hours a day, seven days a week. The idea of finally becoming a dad was the cherry on top. However, I did have reservations about it because of my heart situation, and every now and again I thought about something happening to me and how Rachel would not only be a widow, but a single mom. My son or daughter wouldn't have their father around to raise them.

As exciting as the thought of having a family was, I was equally as frightened at the thought of the worst possible outcome because it was a very real possibility. I didn't focus on it and I didn't wish for it to happen but it was something that was a glaring concern. Nonetheless, I decided to roll with it and let God work it out. The situation was completely out of my control and I couldn't waste any more time playing the "what if" game in my mind. If being a dad and living to see old age was meant to be, then it would be. If not, then okay, I can accept that. But the one thing that was not going to own me was the fear of the unknown. You have to feel the fear because it's there but move past it anyway. Fear is the ultimate enemy of achievement of any kind and it is the best friend of stagnation. I came this far and it was too late to turn back, so forward we go!

December 23, 2012 arrived and it was a cold, dreary, rainy day. We got up and did our last-minute running around to pick up gifts and food from the supermarket to prepare for a small gathering we were having at our home for a few friends on Christmas Day. Each holiday that passed was a milestone for me because there was a time when I didn't think I would see too many of them. Pre-heart condition, I never made a big fuss about the holidays or celebrating my birthday. I mean, I went to parties and such, but I never really planned anything to entertain guests at my house. After we got married, Rachel kind of changed that. She loves to cook and entertain guests, and after going through what I went through with my health challenge, I really began to appreciate the fact that not only was I here to see another holiday, but I could spend it with Rachel and a few close friends. These special moments became more precious to me than receiving gifts; although, I liked receiving gifts, too.

Nightfall came and the day was winding down. We completed all of our shopping and now it was time to just chill out and relax. Rachel made the most delicious meal and we ate dinner. We even had a glass of wine to go with the meal. This was new for me because I'm not a wine drinker. But I figured, what the heck, it's the holidays, I should celebrate and enjoy myself.

We sat in the living room and watched a movie on TV. We talked more about the baby process and started coming up with names for the child. We both were really excited at the thought of becoming parents and finally being a real family. I can only describe that evening as blissful. After the movie went off, we went to bed and decided to catch another movie on Netflix. I believe we only watched a few minutes of it and called it a night. We gave each other a kiss goodnight, looking forward to waking up the next day. Only that didn't happen. After this, I don't remember anything else that transpired.

CHAPTER 14

RACHEL
A DATE WITH FATE

The weekend seemed to fly by. There was never enough time in the day to get everything done. Those were the first thoughts that crossed my mind when I woke up early Sunday morning, December 23, 2012. All I could think about was everything I needed to accomplish as it was the weekend before Christmas.

I did the usual tidy-up to the house, laundry, grocery shopping, and last-minute Christmas shopping. Needless to say, my weekend was full. But there was something different about this day. I can also recall a heaviness in the air; there was not a ray of sunshine at all in the sky. It was one of those skies where you were not sure if it was going to rain, snow, or monsoon. Nothing about it was invigorating or life-giving. The cold in the air was thick and wet. It was certainly one of those winter days that made you want to stay indoors and hibernate under the covers. Running errands was the last thing I wanted to do, but I had to.

Johnnie and I started our Sunday as we normally do. We gave thanks and praise for the blessings we had and were grateful for the life we'd been able to create for ourselves. He had truly been a blessing in my life. Who would have known life with this man could have been so sweet and satisfying? But it was.

As our Sunday progressed, I was home cooking dinner and getting our last-minute gifts wrapped. Johnnie went to the gym to get a quick workout in. When he walked in the back door, I could tell he was on the phone. He was taking with his mother. I recall him sharing with her what his plans were for the holidays and how nice it would have been if she were there spending Christmas with us. Johnnie loves it when his mom comes to visit us. He cherishes those intimate moments with her as he knows time on this earth is short and precious. The only thing I was able to make out from their conversation was that she planned on spending the holidays with us next year and he was happy with that.

As he continued to converse with his mother, I whispered, "Are you hungry? Ready to eat?" He said yes and motioned to me that he was starving! After a workout, he was always ready to eat everything in sight. So, I went to the kitchen, fixed him a plate, and he kindly let his mom know that he was going to eat dinner and that he would talk to her tomorrow. He took his plate into the living room, set a tray in front of him, and ate his dinner as he watched Sunday Night Football. All in all, it was a typical, perfect Sunday evening at home.

I poured him a glass of wine and he took a sip then told me it tasted funny and that he was not interested in drinking the rest. I thought that was a bit odd as I sampled his wine and it tasted fine to me. But I did what any loving wife would do, I took the wine off his hands and drank it myself. He finished eating his meal and drifted off to sleep. The TV eventually started watching him. After he napped for a bit, we went about the rest of our Sunday activities until it was time to turn in for the night. We decided to watch a Netflix movie while lying in bed.

By 3:00 a.m., Christmas Eve, I began to feel myself drift back into reality. I was in such a deep sleep that it took me a moment to realize why and how I was being awakened from my slumber. I could feel myself going back and forth, back and forth, but I was still unclear as to why my body was moving this way. Was I sleeping? Dreaming? It wasn't long before I awoke to feel my husband's arms around me, pulling me back and forth. I immediately jumped up.

"Baby, are you okay?" I asked in a panic. "Baby are you okay?" I repeated. Nothing. I then began to shake him and say, "Baby, wake up. Honey, wake up! You're having a bad dream." Again, nothing. I thought to myself, something is wrong. He's had bad dreams and nightmares before, but I was able to snap him out of it. Not this time.

I jumped out of the bed, went to the edge of our bedroom and turned on the lights, only to see my husband in bed, having convulsion-like seizures, his eyes rolling to the back of his head. At that moment, something came over me. To this day, I cannot explain what it was, but all I know is that I had to immediately act. I ran to the bed, picked up the phone, and called 9-1-1.

"Help!" I yelled into the phone. "Help, please, help, I think my husband is having a heart attack!" These were words I never in my life wanted to have to utter.

By that time, the operator could tell I was beginning to lose it. I was on the bed, watching my husband's body have these uncontrollable convulsions as if the life was being thrusted out of him. She told me that I had to administer CPR until the fire department arrived. At that moment, another click happened. I climbed on top of his body, straddled myself over him, and began giving him chest compressions.

1, 2, 3, 4... 1, 2, 3, 4... 1, 2, 3, 4. That was the rhythm I had to keep while giving him chest compressions. *1, 2, 3, 4... 1, 2, 3, 4... 1, 2, 3, 4.*

Imagine being over the love of your life, with all your energy, heart and might, pumping his chest all the while, crying, praying, yelling, screaming, agonizing because his convulsions are getting less and less, his breathing occurring less and less, as he is becoming more and more lifeless. Then, all of a sudden, while I was giving him chest compressions, everything stopped.

He stopped moving, stopped squirming, stopped quivering, stopped gasping.

He was gone.

Dead.

All I could hear was myself screaming at the 9-1-1 operator. "Where are they? Where are they?" No one had arrived at my house yet. No EMT, no fire department, no police. No one! I screamed again, "Where are they?"

And all I heard yelling back at me was the 9-1-1 operator. "Rachel, keep going!"

And that is what I did. I continued. *1, 2, 3, 4... 1, 2, 3, 4... 1, 2, 3, 4*, as I watched my husband's eyes roll into his head. *1, 2, 3, 4... 1, 2, 3, 4... 1, 2, 3, 4.* His body was lifeless and all I could do was keep doing those compressions.

The enormous amount of energy and love that it took to keep going is beyond comprehension. I began to feel my jaw lock up on me and my entire body felt ready to shut down. My arms felt like they wanted to snap, my back wanting to bend and break. These were the longest ten minutes of my life.

Suddenly, four angels rushed into my house. They yelled for us and I got off my husband and ran to them, frantically showing them where we were.

They immediately stormed into our bedroom, took Johnnie off the bed, and placed his limp body on the floor between our bed and the door leading into our master bathroom. They then began giving him chest compressions, taking over from where I left off.

The only thing I could do at that time was pace in the bathroom. From my vantage point, all I could see was his torso and the angels—firefighters—working on him.

As I paced back and forth in our bathroom while the Fire Rescue team feverishly worked on Johnnie, all I could do was pray. I continued pacing with my hand folded under my chin, praying, as I watched him lying on the floor. I pleaded with God, asking Him for mercy. I prayed and cried for a miracle. It was all that I could do.

At that point, one of the firefighters placed a defibrillator pad on his chest and I heard, "Clear!" as a jolt lifted his body from the floor. I prayed some more but nothing happened. I began praying again, and then I heard, "Clear!" once more. His body jolted again and again, but still, nothing. This happened four more times. By then, I could only squeeze my hands tighter and close my eyes as if that would ensure God would hear my prayer. Then everything stopped.

I slowly walked to the doorway, pulling every ounce of courage I could muster to see what was going on. I saw my beloved's body on the floor as one firefighter kneeled at his head with an apparatus helping him breathe. His chest was going up and down. He was breathing! My eyes scanned up to his and they were still lifeless. My gaze was interrupted by a voice that said, "Ma'am, his heart is beating again. We must get him to the hospital ASAP."

According to the firemen, it was uncommon to continue reviving someone after six attempts and no life response occurs, but in this case, they decided to keep going and defeat the odds. I can't even express the level of love and gratitude I have that they did.

By this time, my house was swarming with people. The EMTs had arrived and drilled a hole in his leg just below his left knee. There was blood all over the carpet. That was how they were able to deliver life-saving medicine to him since his veins had collapsed from his heart not beating. The police were in my house as well, trying to assess what was going on. They placed him on a gurney and began to wheel him into an ambulance.

I had to act quickly because I could not allow him to be out of my sight. In such a panicked state, I took a pair of yoga pants and a sweatshirt out of the hamper and put them on. I had the presence of mind to take my purse, cell phone, cell phone charger, and keys.

As I was walking out the door, next to Johnnie, my neighbor came over and asked what had happened. I told him Johnnie had a heart attack and we were on our way to the hospital now. I didn't know the difference between a heart attack and sudden cardiac arrest at the time, even though I heard Dr. Jones mention it from the last visit with him. All I knew was that his heart was not working properly.

By 3:45 a.m., we pulled into the hospital and it felt like a scene from *Grey's Anatomy*. The medical staff greeted us at the ambulance and wheeled him into the emergency room. I followed beside him with every intention of not letting him out of my sight.

I remember vividly looking at him but not seeing any life in his half-opened eyes. As he was brought into an examination room, I recall a slew of people attaching all sorts of machines to his body. The lights and the beeping sound from the machines were beginning to overwhelm me when someone from the medical staff asked me exactly what happened. As I shared with them the events that took place, they asked if he had any of those highly-caffeinated drinks that elevate your heartrate and I said that he didn't. They also asked me what medications he was taking and I shared with them what I knew. While the interrogation was taking place, my eyes never left his body. One of the hospital staff asked if we had family nearby. It was at that moment, I had this uncontrollable feeling of helplessness as the word "no", came out of my mouth. I was barely audible when she asked me the same question again and I said, "No! We don't have any family nearby, it's just us." I was all he had and he was all I had as well.

At that moment, another attendant came and told me that they needed to continue to work on him and that I had to leave. It was at that point, I felt myself losing it. I said, "No, I can't leave him", with a stream of hot tears flowing from my eyes. I felt my legs go numb and my knees buckle as two people grabbed me and escorted me from his examination room. I had a hopeless feeling in the pit of my stomach. This must be what hell feels like because my agony could not get any worse. I was escorted into a waiting room where two of my neighbors were waiting. I was shocked to see our neighbors there. It was as if God knew I needed someone there for support. He had sent me two of the kindest men I knew to help Johnnie and I in this moment.

The doctor came into the waiting area and asked if I had notified other members of our family. I told them that I hadn't yet. The nurse said that it may be a good time to call them. As I sat down, my next-door neighbor sat to my left, the other to my right, and I let out a gut-wrenching scream. I was in so much pain, it was unbearable. My neighbors tried to console me, but there was no amount of consoling in the world that could stop my heart from breaking. My heart ached like it had never ached before. How was I going to tell his mom? I was stuck between the proverbial rock and hard place.

I finally pulled out my cell phone and made the first call. It was to my mother. Call me selfish, but the little girl in me needed her mommy. I wanted her by my side to tell me it was going to be okay. "Mom," I said, sobbing, "I need you."

She asked what had happened and I told her as best as I could. I heard her say that she was on her way. My mom lives in Georgia, so it was a three-and-a-half-hour drive for her to get to Charlotte. I knew that no matter what was going on, I needed her to take care of me so that I could take care of Johnnie.

Once I ended my call with her, I felt a sliver of this massive burden being lifted from my chest. Her voice and knowing that she was on her way gave me the courage to make the second phone call. This time, I had to call Johnnie's sister in New Jersey.

The phone rang and rang, until, finally, she answered the phone. "Hello, Peewee, this is Rachel." I was crying and from the tone of my voice, she knew immediately that something terrible happened to Johnnie.

"Oh, no, what happened?" she yelled. "Don't tell me that Johnnie is gone," she said.

"No, but Johnnie is in the hospital. It looks like he had a heart attack." I went on to tell her that he had died but was brought back to life. There was a moment of silence; I guess she was still processing all that I was sharing with her so early in the morning.

At that moment, I looked up and saw our neighbors, Gary and Zeke, looking back at me with pain in their eyes. They knew how hard this was for me to deal with. It was as if they wanted to take away the pain and anguish.

The shock overtook Johnnie's sister and she remained speechless. "Hello, hello? Are you there?"

"Yes," she finally responded. "Yes, I'm still here. Where is he? Can I talk to him?" I told her that he had not yet regained consciousness. His heart was beating, but he did not appear to be alive. He was in some sort of coma. It took her a while to digest all of the details I was sharing with her. This was not the kind of call she was expecting to hear on Christmas Eve, which also happened to be her birthday.

"Peewee, we have to tell your mom. She needs to know, but I don't have the courage or strength to tell her. My heart cannot take what her reaction might be." We talked about our concern regarding how their mom was going to handle receiving such a blow. Her forty-year-old son, who is the apple of her eye, was in the hospital because his heart stopped beating. He had died but was brought back to life and was now in God-knows-what condition.

We ended our call and I had a bit of relief because my soul could not bear to have to break this news to my mother-in-law. I sighed and took a deep breath.

As I sat in a slumped position, replaying the events that occurred in our bedroom in my mind, I heard, "Mrs. Davis?"

In a fog, I raised my head and replied, "Yes?" The doctor walked toward me, and I had a sinking feeling in my chest that what he was going to share would shake me to my core forever.

"Your husband is on life support and has not regained consciousness. He suffered Sudden Cardiac Arrest and is in critical condition. The next forty-eight hours are crucial as he is not out of the woods yet. We started a cold-cool process where we are freezing his body to hypothermic levels in an attempt to salvage brain function. Because your husband was gone for so long without a pulse, we are not sure if he received adequate oxygen to his brain, therefore, we are unable to determine if he will survive. If he does, we're unclear on what his brain capacity could be. Mrs. Davis, I need you to understand that the man you know as your husband may never be the same, and there is a strong possibility he will not come out of this. If he does, he could potentially be in a vegetative state.

"Mrs. Davis, we've done all that we can do to save your husband. Mrs. Davis? Do you understand what I just said?" I replied with a low and meek "yes" then swallowed what felt like a brick in my chest. "Mrs. Davis, are you a praying woman?" the doctor asked. I replied again, "yes," again and then he said, "I suggest you pray. There is nothing else we can do for him."

"Can I see him?" I asked.

"Of course," he replied. "Right this way."

I entered my husband's hospital room only to be confronted with a sight that will never be erased from my memory.

CHAPTER 15

THE POWER OF PRAYER

I gasped as I took in the sight of my husband lying there. The room was dimly-lit. I remember feeling a chill in the air as I made my way to his bed. It took a while for my mind to comprehend what I was looking at. He was lying there looking like he was sleeping with tubes coming out of his nose, mouth, and throat. The beeps of three monitors that were displaying his vitals broke the silence in the room.

I walked over to him and just stood by his bedside, staring, analyzing every square-inch of his body. He was lying flat on his back, eyes closed, covered from his neck to his toes. I touched his hand and it was cold as ice. I leaned over and kissed his forehead, then kissed his cheek and lips. I guess I was hoping for some kind of response. My kisses would always get a reaction from him, but this time, nothing. Not a flinch, not a smile, not a wink, nothing.

Mrs. Davis, are you a praying woman?

I heard the echo of the doctor's voice in the back of my head and I thought, *yes, yes, of course, I am a praying woman.* It was at that moment that I began to pray. I prayed so hard, I began sobbing, the tears streaming down my face as my eyes started to sting. In the midst of my heartfelt, gut-wrenching prayer with God, I looked

116

over at my husband and heard, "Two or more." I froze. Matthew 18:20 came to mind. "For where two or three gather in my name, there am I with them."

I picked up the phone and made a call to the one person I knew that could quickly reach out to as many people as he possibly could to pray for Johnnie.

Rob was not only one of Johnnie's very good friends, but also his business partner. When I called him at such an early hour in the morning, he knew something was amiss. I explained everything that had happened. I got to a point where I was so emotional I had to leave the room because I did not want Johnnie—in case he could hear me—to hear that I was getting as emotional as I was.

I remember telling Rob that I needed everyone to pray for a Christmas miracle. He listened, he consoled, and he was on it. He went straight to social media with the news and in a matter of minutes, my phone began to ring. People from all over were calling: friends, colleagues, business partners, even his Pastor from New Jersey. I quickly became overwhelmed with everyone wanting to know about Johnnie's condition and how he was doing. I hadn't quite thought about that.

Johnnie had always been a private man. Despite the fact that I wanted everyone praying, I worried that Rob had shared the news with the world on such a public forum.

The calls continued to come in. People were so concerned and wanting to know more about his condition that folks called every hospital in Charlotte until they found the one he was in. I had to put my phone down because I needed to give him my undivided attention, and shortly after that, people were calling the nurses station asking to speak to me.

I was overwhelmed with exhaustion and seeing my mom as she stood in the doorway of his room gave me a feeling of relief in knowing that I was no longer going to have to endure this on my own. As I sat there looking at her looking at him, I could read the shock and disbelief on her face. It's one thing to hear what was going on, but another thing entirely to enter the intensive care unit in the hospital and witness Johnnie's condition for herself.

She quickly moved to his bedside where I was standing and held me, hugged me, kissed me, and consoled me. God knows I needed my mom with me during this time.

We sat in his room and just watched. We paced back and forth as a means to try and stay calm. Watching him and pacing back and forth was all that we could do. As the nurse and doctors had told us, it was a waiting game, so we had to be patient and wait it out.

Thoughts were racing through my mind that would not allow me to be still. When the nurse came into his room to check his numbers, I asked her what the likelihood of him hearing me was. She calmly and lovingly looked at me and said that he was still alive and that talking to him would not hurt. In fact, he may be able to hear me and it could possibly make things better for him.

After hearing that, I motioned to him, leaned in close to his ear and began to whisper how much I loved him, how much I needed him, how much I wanted him, and how lonely this existence on earth would be without out him. I continued to tell him that he was my hero, my champion, my lion, and my rock. I told him how strong and powerful he is and how the world needed him. I continued to say these words to him over and over again. I told him his heart was functioning at 100% and that he was better than ever before.

I repeated these affirmations to him in hopes that he not only heard me, but could feel me. Even though he did not move or show any signs that he could, I did not stop because I knew deep down my words and my love had the power to penetrate where he was and that that power would bring him back to me.

Minutes seemed like hours and hours seem like days. There was still no change and he did not wake up. I recall the nurse lowering the head of his bed and he opened his eyes. I ran and screamed that he was waking up and they told me, "No, Mrs. Davis, it's just a reflex, a bodily reaction. He is still in a comatose state." Despite it all, I kept the faith and continued whispering words of life, power, and love into his ear, hoping and praying he heard me.

As time passed, more people were calling my phone wanting to know what was going on with him and how he was doing. I became numb to the phone calls and could not focus on them. Sharing his prognosis over and over again was wearing me out and I just could not do it anymore.

The one plus was having family there to shoulder the blow and offer comfort at the same time. My aunt and cousin arrived that afternoon, my sister-in-law that evening. Having them around, although there was nothing they could do to take the pain away from my heart, offered comfort. There was nothing like having family around when you needed them the most.

As the evening approached, Johnnie gave us a scare again. He had a horrible reaction to a medication that they gave him and he started to crash. The machines were beeping all at the same time and there was a flood of white coats— doctors and nurses—rushing into his room.

"Mrs. Davis, we are going to have to ask you to leave," is all I heard. I told them I wasn't leaving and demanded to know what was going on. As I was asking, they rolled in a crash cart and panic started to set in the pit of my stomach again. The doctor said again, "Mrs. Davis we are going to have to ask you to leave. This may not turn out okay, and it would be best if you were outside of the room." My mom and aunt, one on each side, held me up as we walked out of the room. I clasped my hands together and prayed. I prayed like my life depended on it because, at that point, it did.

My mom found a chair in the hallway of the hospital and sat me down as I was on the brink of collapsing. All I could do was hold my hands together, close my eyes as tightly as I could, and pray. I begged God to heed my prayer and spare his life.

After a few minutes, the commotion of what was taking place in the hospital room died down and I was allowed back inside. We walked into his room like nothing ever happen. This was the second time in less than twenty-four hours that his life was spared.

CHAPTER 16

THE POWER OF A PRAYING MOTHER

Later that evening, my sister-in-law arrived from New Jersey. It was Christmas Eve, her birthday, and she spent the majority of her day trying to get a last-minute flight to Charlotte to see her brother. By the time she arrived at the hospital, I was exhausted, completely and emotionally spent, but was happy to see someone from his family making it down. As you would imagine, coming from New Jersey with the holiday among us was a hugely daunting task.

Shortly after her arrival, one of Johnnie's childhood friends arrived as well. Everyone was in shock at seeing him lying there. But I was just happy they made it because the more people that he loved and could love on him, the better. My thought was, if he could feel the love, maybe he would come back to us.

Peewee walked up to him, lying there lifeless in the bed and hooked up to machines and stared at him. She noticed how his skin color had changed to a deep, dark purple like an eggplant. She touched his hand and commented on how cold it was. I explained to her as best I could what the cold-cool procedure was, and that they were trying to preserve whatever brain function he had left. He was actually in the process of warming back up as she touched him. She stopped the doctor and introduced herself as his sister. She asked him if Johnnie still had any brain stem activity. The doctor responded without hesitation and told her that yes, there was. The doctor went on to say that if he recovered, he would need extensive therapy to learn how to walk and speak again. He didn't seem optimistic because of how long it was taking Johnnie to wake up.

If it were up to me, I would have spent the night in the hospital as I did not want to leave Johnnie's bedside, not even for a second. But it was at the behest of the nursing staff as well as family members that I go home, even if just for a few hours to shower and get some rest. I reluctantly left his bedside, leaving him in the care of family and friends, since there was nothing more I could do. His childhood friend, JaModd, drove me home and all I could remember was a feeling of guilt that I had left him alone in the hospital. I walked into the house and, as soon as I walked passed our bedroom door, I started screaming. The agony of seeing the bed and the place on the floor where they worked on him was just too much to handle.

My mom held me up as I lost all feeling in my legs and was on the brink of collapse. Everyone quickly rushed to my side and my aunt handed me a glass of water to help calm me down. Luckily for me, my aunt and mom went to our house earlier and was able to fix the bed and clean up the blood to make things look normal. Despite their efforts, it did not work. I was rushed back to what took place in our bedroom in the wee hours of the morning.

There comes a point in time where being strong is the only option you have and I was at that point. I knew that the only way I was going to get through this was to get it together and conjure up the strength of God. That was a pivotal moment for me.

As we sat in the dark living room, everyone watching me and afraid to move because for fear of my fragile mental and emotional state, I stood up, walked into our bedroom and looked around. Then I walked into our bathroom and looked around. I realized that everything was going to be okay and that I did not need to fear. There was a feeling of peace that overtook me. I went from being fearful to being certain. Everything was going to be okay.

After this ordeal, I took a hot shower, got dressed, came out into the living room, and joined everyone in waiting. Exhaustion finally took over. I was able to close my eyes and fall asleep for a few hours. God knows I needed the rest because Johnnie was not out of the woods yet.

Christmas day arrived and everything was relatively quiet aside from the beeps from the machines that was keeping my husband alive. He was still in a coma and not showing any signs of progress nor was he showing signs of decline. In my estimation, that was a good thing.

That day must have been the longest day in my life. I just sat there watching the clock and whispering affirmations into my husband's ear, sharing stories and memories of private and intimate times together in hopes of him coming back to me. The phone calls were still coming in as well as more visitors. We were truly blessed to have such an outpour of love from our neighbors and friends. People brought food to the hospital, sent cards, flowers, etc. Johnnie even had a fraternity brother who did not know him, but heard what happened, come by to visit and pray with me. Acts of kindness like that truly makes a grim situation brighter.

As the hours passed, we were waiting on his mother to come. Since it was Christmas, she was unable to find a fight out of New Jersey to get to Charlotte in time, so she and Rocky, my husband's baby brother, caught the train to Charlotte.

I remember clear as day the moment Johnnie's mother arrived. I was sitting by his side, looking at him, then out of the corner of my eye, I saw a petite woman standing in the doorway. Her energy was so magnetic, I knew right then and there, my mother-in-law had arrived. I stood up and ran to her and gave her a hug. I knew it was not easy seeing her son lying there in that bed, connected to a machine that was keeping him alive. I knew she needed support, the same support that was given to me when my mom arrived. We hugged each other as she stood there, staring at her son in silence. I stepped back a few steps to give her a moment to take everything in. She dropped her bag to the floor, took off her coat, and let it fall to the floor as we walked toward his bed.

She stood beside him, stretched her arm over her son's body, and began to pray in a manner that only a God-fearing woman could do. She prayed and prayed and prayed, never dropping her arms, never wavering and never losing the intensity in her voice. When she was done praying, she sat down in the chair on the left side of his body. She did not utter a word, she just looked at him as she rocked her body back and forth. I sat to the right of him, watching over him as I had done since this whole ordeal began. She grabbed his hand and rubbed it between hers as a means to warm him. She watched over him with loving eyes as she rocked back and forth, praying to God for her son to come back to her.

Johnnie's mom and I sat there for several minutes after she finished praying for him. All I could think was, God, please hear our prayers because we need him here. *I* need him! Shortly after that, I could not believe what I was seeing with my own eyes!

Oh my God, oh my God!

"Mom, look, he opened his eyes!" I yelled as I jumped out of my chair and ran over to him. His eyes were open! I looked at the clock and it read 11:53 p.m.! God did it, yes, He did! I prayed for my Christmas miracle and Johnnie opened his eyes at 11:53 p.m. on Christmas Day! His mom and I were elated. Words could not express the amount of joy we experienced in that moment. It must have been no more than fifteen minutes since she began praying over him, and in that time, our prayers were answered. God showed that miracles still do come down from heaven above.

My husband opened his eyes! I cried, but this time, they were tears of joy, amazement, and gratitude. The nurse and doctors come rushing into his room to see what all the commotion was about and I yelled that he'd opened his eyes! It took Johnnie a little while to comprehend what was going on. The last thing he remembered was going to bed and then waking up in a hospital room, wondering what had happened.

Once the rest of the family heard he was awake, everyone came rushing in to witness the good news, to witness our Christmas miracle. We were so ecstatic that he pulled through despite the bleak odds stacked against him that there was not a dry eye in the room. We were hugging on him and loving on him. This was, by far, the absolute best Christmas gift God could have ever given us. But in the midst of everyone's joy and jubilation, I looked over at Johnnie and he had this look of utter confusion on his face. His eyes were wide open, dazed, and confused. It was as if he was trying to speak with his eyes, asking what was going on. I told everyone to quiet down and leave for the moment because I needed to calm him down and orient him. Even the doctors said there was too much stimulation and that he needed to rest. From his expression, it was apparent he had no idea what had happened or how he ended up in the hospital.

I immediately recalled the doctors telling me he may not remember and that the next couple of days after waking up from his coma were critical in assessing if any brain damage had taken place. I asked him if he knew who I was and he said, yes. I told him that he suffered cardiac arrest and that he was in the hospital. When I gave him that response, he had a look of shock on his face.

A few seconds passed before he asked me the same question, and I gave him the same answer. A few seconds would pass again and he would ask me the same question and I would give him the same answer. This went on for hours. At one point, when it started to sink in what I was saying, he asked me the same question again then he began to cry uncontrollably. My heart ached to see him react in such a way.

Johnnie continued doing this until I finally asked the doctor what was going on. He reassured me that this was a normal response and that the next hurdle we would have to cross would be to make sure he was cognitively sound. In order to determine his brain functionality, he would have to answer a couple of questions; his name, date of birth, what year we were in, and who the President of the United States was. Needless to say, I began practicing those questions immediately. There was no way I was going to accept anyone telling me my husband, Johnnie Davis, was not 100% healed. I would talk to him as much as I could, as often as I could, sharing memories of our life together. I was elated each time he told me he remembered. My heart leaped for joy because my husband was returning to me. He passed the cognitive assessment with flying colors and was on the mend.

With each day that passed, he was getting better and better. He was able to receive visitors and he thoroughly enjoyed having them. Johnnie had friends from all over the northeast make their way to Charlotte to see him and spend time with him. It was awesome to see the outpour of love he received; to see how people whose lives he touched, traveled from near and far to see the man that defied the odds, cheated death, and came to on Christmas day. Even the firefighters who were the first response team came to see him. These firemen from Station 38 are not just civic servants, to us, they are family.

I really knew that he was "back" when he requested that I go home to bring him his clippers so that he could cut his hair. Johnnie did not like the fact that his gray hairs were showing nor did he like the way he smelled. So, yes, I had to bring his cologne, too. You have to really know who he is to truly understand why this was so funny.

After surviving death by sudden cardiac arrest and being pulseless and without oxygen for well over sixteen minutes, he still had the presence of mind to take care of his hair and hygiene.

After shaving his head and face, he turned to me and said, "Babe, how old do you think I look?" I just bust out in laughter because that's something he would frequently ask me anyway.

I responded, "Babe, I don't know. All I know is that you look great! It's much better to see you standing upright on your own two feet as opposed to lying flat on your back with tubes coming out of every orifice of your body."

With a smile on his face, he said, "Yeah, you're right about that. But I still look thirty-five, right?" I thought to myself, this man is something else.

After he finished beautifying himself, he had to learn how to regain his balance and go walking with the nurses on the floor. They wanted to make sure his equilibrium was reset and that he could walk freely without falling. He looked at me and said, "Babe, I feel like a puppy. I have to go for a walk. Wow, okay, let's do it." He walked around the entire nurses station with his legs shaking like a newborn baby fawn. He found it quite amusing that he had to learn how to walk again. He eventually figured it out and began walking around on his own with no assistance. I cried tears of joy watching him because it wasn't that long ago that he was laying under my outstretched hands, dead. In that moment, I realized the miracle that God performed and I was overwhelmed with joy.

In the quiet moments, early on during this ordeal, I kept steadfast and close to my heart two things. First, the fact that God would grant us a Christmas miracle and that Johnnie would open his eyes and wake from him coma on Christmas day. Second, he would walk out of the hospital before the New Year. Everyone I spoke to, if they were not in accordance with these two affirmations, I did not talk to them. If they were not in agreement of total healing and restoration, I would not have them in my presence or his. I was that steadfast, unapologetic, and unreasonable when it came to the energy and mindset I wanted, *needed*, around us.

Because of the amount of faith we'd exercised, and the amount of personal development we'd gone through, I knew the power of positive energy and positive thoughts. It was imperative to have the right energy around him.

It was December 31, 2012, Johnnie and I were lying next to one another in his hospital bed, watching the festivities taking place in Times Square as one million people gathered to celebrate and usher in the New Year. As I turned my eyes away from the television to look at the sweet face of my wonderful and amazing husband, I was consumed with an overwhelming feeling of gratitude. There is not a word in the English language strong enough or descriptive enough to describe how grateful and happy I was. I looked in his eyes and smiled; he smiled back. I glossed my eyes over his face, his neck, and rested them on his chest. I was grateful for the bandage that covered the scar that represented the device he had implanted in his chest earlier that day. I was also grateful for the doctor's assurance that, with the device in his chest, nothing like this would ever happen again.

He looked over at me and said, "Babe, we should watch the ball drop next year."

I stared at him, smiled, and said, "Yes, we can watch the ball drop on New Year's Eve for the rest of our lives."

The next day, we walked out of the hospital in true Johnnie Davis fashion, feeling ten feet tall and bullet proof. He was excited and grateful to be alive yet nervous and unsure of what was to come. The one thing that was certain, I had my husband back, and I was going to do everything in my power to ensure he lived a long, fulfilled, and healthy life. As we sat in the car, I looked over at him. He looked at me and I said, "You have come a long way. God really has something special planned for you with your life. You are a walking miracle! Let's go, baby. Let's go home".

CHAPTER 17
JOHNNIE
THE BEGINNING OF A NEW LIFE

I was discharged from the hospital on January 1, 2013 and I couldn't remember the way home. Rachel was driving and I didn't recognize where we were. I had driven on this very same highway thousands of times, yet I had no idea where I was. I was afraid that maybe I did suffer some brain damage after all.

I had no recollection of what happened to me during the month of December. It was as if the files in my head had been erased from my memory. When we pulled up to our cul-de-sac and approached our house, I didn't recognize the house either. It felt like home but I just didn't remember it. Rachel held my hand as I walked inside and looked around, trying to reconnect with my surroundings, but I felt nothing. I saw our pictures on the coffee table and knew I obviously lived there but nothing was coming back to me.

As the days went by, my memory returned and I did feel at home again, but it was scary for a while. I guess my brain had to reboot itself. After all, I was pulseless and without oxygen for over sixteen minutes. It was a blessing that my brain was still functioning at all. God is still in the miracle business!

I had an ICD implanted in my chest and my arm was in a sling to prevent me from making any sudden movements or raising my arm above my head. I had two wires screwed into my heart and the scar tissue had to form around them so that they would stay intact. Any sudden movements could potentially rupture the incision where the leads were and that was not a good thing because that would kill me for sure. I was very weak and had little to no energy. My heart function was around 15% or so. I was right back to where I was seven years prior, only this time, I had a device in my chest to prevent me from going into sudden cardiac arrest again.

I was taking eight pills a day, which made me miserable. I was reliving the same situation that I had worked so hard to avoid. I focused all of my energy on getting well and made sure that I kept a positive mindset. Dr. Jones had told me a while back that this was likely to happen and he was 100% spot on. I did go into cardiac arrest and I did die. The mere thought of it to this day makes me teary-eyed because I can't believe I'm still alive.

I learned one extremely valuable lesson from this whole experience and that is you are not in control of anything. I had no control at all. I had done all that I could to prevent this from happening and it still did. I died but my life was spared and I came back to life. I wasn't going to beat myself up over anything this time because it was out of my hands.

I was in a medically-induced coma for two days and I told Rachel about my experience on the other side. I don't know when my spirit left my body but I do recall feeling a sense of pure joy, love, peace, and tranquility and it was perfectly overwhelming. I remember feeling like I did not want to return from where I was because that place was perfect. I did not see a light or a long tunnel, but I heard a distinct voice that was so subtle, but loud and clear. It said to me, "It's not your time. You have to go back." It was as if time stood still and nothing moved. It was perfectly peaceful and I didn't want to return, but I had to, and I did.

At first, I wasn't going to tell anyone about my experience because I didn't want to look like I was crazy or something. But the more I talked about it, the better I felt, and the more I realized that my experience was not just for me, but for everyone. I had to share it because people needed to know that God is real and that He's still in the miracle business. When I came home, I had a choice to make. I could either be depressed about what transpired or rejoice in the fact that I was still alive. I didn't know why it happened, I only knew that it did. I didn't know why my life was spared, only that it was. It must have been spared for a reason and I was determined to discover the answer.

Only 5% of sudden cardiac arrest victims actually survive and I was one of the blessed 5%. I realized that, despite me suffering the sudden cardiac arrest, I was given a huge gift. When you pass onto the next realm, life as you know it will be over and there will be no more pain or suffering. The feeling that I felt in that space is one that I long to feel again someday when my time is up. I no longer fear death because I know it's not the end. It's the beginning of a new existence where you reach your highest self. It's the place or part of you that I believe all men aspire to achieve, but for a multitude of reasons, are so distracted my menial differences and separated by ego that they miss the true essence of what it means to have life. Life is meant to create as much joy and spread as much love for your fellow man for all your days. It's a gift that I will continue sharing with as many people as I can and I'm grateful for the experience. I was given the gift of knowing for certain that God is indeed real.

Despite that, there was still a very long road ahead because I had to develop my strength again. I had gone through this process before and it was quite arduous to say the least. I had a difficult time wrapping my head around having this foreign metal device in my chest. It somehow made it official that my heart just wasn't right. I mean, I already knew that, but part of me was still in denial about it. But I didn't let it hold me down. I returned to positive thinking, which I believe was the main reason why I never experienced depression as many heart patients do. My mind wouldn't allow me to dwell on the negative because I had trained it not to. I learned to block out all things negative, including negative people, because your subconscious mind records and stores everything. When you compile negative thought on top of negative thought, it can bury you into a deep, dark hole that most people never escape from and they require medication to help them deal with it. There was no way I was going to allow that to happen to me. I approached this with the same mindset that I did when I suffered congestive heart failure. I told myself that I was going to beat this and it would not control or consume me. It would not own me, I would own it. It would not stop me from doing all of the things that I desired in life. I just had to figure out how to make it all happen.

While this battle was taking place in my head, I still had the problem of having very low energy. My taste buds didn't work and I couldn't walk 100 feet and back without getting tired. I also had an epiphany about my business. I no longer wanted to participate in the legal services industry. Something happened to me that I cannot explain when I came back to my body. I came back a different person and it was as if all of the things that I did before didn't matter anymore. The old me really did die and a new version of me was born. The desire and zeal that I had for doing that business just left me. The only challenge was I didn't know what else I wanted to do. That's the only business I had known the past eleven years. I never thought about doing anything else outside of my real estate venture. Everything was back on track with it and things were moving in the right direction. Yet, still, I had no desire to continue with it. I was in a serious quandary and I needed some direction because I didn't know what I was going to do next.

Seismologists say that when an earthquake is taking place below the ocean, the earth's crust is shifting and this can cause a tsunami. The shifting of the crusts is not a smooth shift like going from first to second gear in a sports car, but rather a violent shift where it seems that the gears in the car are going against each other, causing a massive disruption in the car's ability to go forward. When the earth's crusts shift, they are actually grinding against each other in the opposite direction, creating an unimaginable amount of force that causes the entire ocean to move, which results in catastrophic damage to anything and everything in its path. I didn't know it at the time, but when I said that I something in me had changed and I no longer wanted to do my previous business, a tsunami was headed my way. My heart was in bad shape, I had no energy. I didn't want to do my business anymore and I had no idea what I wanted to do going forward.

Soon after my epiphany, several of my key leaders decided they were going to jump ship and head to another company. No one said anything to me, they all just decided to leave at the same time. After years of building together, countless trips, seminars, trainings, etc., it all just slowly imploded. I watched my income start to dwindle little by little. Meanwhile, I could not get back out there and hit the streets because I was still impaired physically. God was setting me up for something much greater but I didn't see it at the time. Little did I know, that was only the beginning.

I called my doctor's office one day to tell him that I had this metallic taste in my mouth and that my sense of smell was off. I didn't know what that was and it scared the crap out of me. I spoke with my cardiologist and he told me that the metallic taste in my mouth was a result of taking the medications. He said all medication is toxic but there was one drug in particular that I was taking that was "highly" toxic. It stabilized my heart rhythm, basically slowing it down so that it wouldn't beat out of rhythm, but simultaneously, it was destroying my liver and kidneys. He said that I couldn't stay on this particular prescription longer than three months because it was too dangerous. Virtually, I was taking poison which was fixing one problem but causing another.

"Doc, how can I rid my body of the harmful toxins because I don't want to have to take medication for my liver and kidneys, especially when there is nothing wrong with them? I'm already taking so much medication as it is. What can I do?"

"I don't know," he said. "Perhaps, you can drink a lot of water and flush it out that way." I thought to myself, that's it? Drink a lot of water? You're a board-certified, well-respected cardiologist in the Carolina medical community and this is your best answer? What the fuck? I was highly annoyed, disturbed, and, yes, pissed off with his response because I was looking for something a little more sophisticated, I guess. I was especially pissed because it appeared that my whole world was just unraveling in front of me and there was nothing I could do to stop it. My health was going in the wrong direction, my business was being ripped from under me, my medications were helping but they were highly toxic and killing me slowly, and I had no idea what to do! All of this came crashing down on me all at once and I felt like I was going to lose my mind. I prayed to God and asked Him why He brought me back to this? What was I supposed to do now? I knew He didn't bring me this far to leave me. I needed guidance on this one because I didn't know what to do.

One day, I was sitting in the living room thinking about what my next steps were going to be and an idea came to me, the same as it did when I had my first heart episode. Instead of saying woe is me, why me, what now, I had to ask myself empowering questions. So, the question to myself was what can I do to help improve my health first? That was paramount because without improving my health, nothing else really mattered. I can't do anything without it, so I needed to start there.

I walked into the kitchen to get something to eat and came across Rachel's products that she had ordered a few months prior from Isagenix. Although I'd initially thought the products were used for weight loss, I discovered that they were also good for flooding the body with minerals and nutrients that were missing from our food supply. I picked up a bottle that said *Cleanse for Life*. I had no idea what it was but the name made sense to me. I needed to cleanse my body of all the harmful toxins from the medications I was taking.

At this point, I had nothing to lose by trying them, so I dove right in and began using everything she had in her box. When I told Rachel what I had done, she almost hit the ceiling! I thought she would be happy that I took the initiative to help myself but she wasn't. She was scared because she didn't know how it would affect me with all the medications I was already taking. I assured her that not only was this all-natural, but it was also the best superfood I could put in my system. After all, that's all it was, just food not medicine. I told her what I'd read about the products. I didn't really know for myself, I just sounded like I knew what I was talking about!

My first seven days of using the products, I noticed that my body had released five pounds around my stomach area and I was beginning to see my top two abdominal muscles. That was awesome because I hadn't seen them since college and I wondered where they had gone.

Three more weeks went by and I lost another eighteen pounds of toxic fat from my body. I couldn't believe what was happening. And not only was I losing weight, I also gained an insane amount of energy, which is exactly what I wanted and needed the most.

February came and I had a new pep in my step. I felt better and more alive. Despite everything going on around me, I knew something good was happening on the inside. The more I used the products, the better I felt, and this had never happened to me before with anything else. On the business front, I was still in a quandary because I didn't know what I was going to do about that. As I mentioned earlier, key leaders had left and more were leaving. What took me twelve years to build only took a few months to destroy, and although I began feeling better, I still wasn't quite strong enough to get back out there.

One of Rachel's good friends asked if she had ever seen the compensation plan for Isagenix. She knew we were veteran networkers with a large team and thought we would be great at building in this company. We both declined. Though we loved the products, we didn't want to work for the company. We were programmed not to do business with companies like Isagenix because it was considered a "me, too" company, meaning there were so many other companies offering the same or similar products. It was just congested with competition.

Meanwhile, we thought we had the best deal in town because it wasn't product-based nor did we have any competition. That was embedded deep in our minds and it was hard to let that go. Many people miss out on great opportunities because it goes against their mental programming and we almost did the same thing. Thankfully, her other friend, Tracie, who later became our lifeboat in the midst of the Tsunami, came back to us and asked if she could arrange a meeting with us and the top income earner in our area. I asked Rachel, what if this is the change we have been looking for?

I knew I wanted to do something different business-wise and Rachel was ready for something new as well. She never really said anything to me about it because she supported me in whatever it is I wanted to do. But I know she knew long before any of this happened that our time was over in our previous company. Her intuition was correct once again. I said to her, "What do we constantly say in our trainings? A wise man investigates what a fool takes for granted. So, let's just go and see what it is. If we are not interested, we can say thanks but no thanks and leave it there."

We agreed to meet with the top income earners in the area to see what the opportunity entailed. It was a new month and I was ready to learn something. I can recall being in so much pain on the way there because the incision from my heart surgery was still tender and I was taking pain killers to numb the pain. Boy, was that an uncomfortable ride to their home. Nonetheless, I fought through it because I wanted to see what this was all about.

While sitting at the dining room table, learning about this incredible new business, my chest was throbbing. I sat there listening as intently as I could before I just kind of zoned out. I saw their lips moving but I didn't hear anything coming out of their mouths. I tried my best to block out the pain but all of my attempts were in vain. My legs began shaking and I tapped Rachel underneath the table to signal her to give me my pain killers.

She looked at me and saw that I was suffering and she quietly put the medicine in my hand under the table. I quickly clenched my fist around it. We didn't want them to know that I had just had heart surgery and was recovering from a near-death incident. After all, I wanted to make a really good first impression. I asked for a glass of water, and as soon as I could sneak and take the pills without them seeing me, I did so. I felt weird about it later, though. I wasn't sure why I needed to hide the fact that I'd just had surgery the month before. No need in being all weird about it.

After a while, the pain began to subside and I was able to pay attention. I really didn't understand everything that they showed us, however, I saw enough to the point where it made sense to me. Herb explained more about how the compensation plan worked and then he did something that most businessmen never do. He showed us the money! We didn't ask him do it, but we appreciated him for doing so, despite the fact that we were sitting in the evidence of their success.

Their palatial home was exquisite and the decor was something out of a *Better Homes* magazine. He didn't believe in the concept of "fake it, till you make it", which was a common theme in our industry of network marketing. These beautiful people were, and are, the real deal. After we saw the potential of the opportunity provided, we decided to make a transition and join the health and wellness movement. It was perfect timing in a sense because I really wanted to do something different with my life. I believe that this was all part of a divine plan, and we kindly just went with the flow.

After meeting with them for several hours, we knew that we had seen something very special and that this was our invitation to get back on track. I saw how I could improve my health as well as create something even bigger and better than before. God was right on time as usual. Each major obstacle that was presented before me, He made it possible for me to make it to safety. I also learned that I didn't know what I didn't know and that you will miss out on a blessing of a lifetime when your mind is closed. I believe that I had to go through my ordeal in order to get to the point where I could have an open mind to do something different. I was so locked in to my previous company and my old belief system that I literally had to die to be taken away from it.

Rachel and I embarked on this new journey together, but we had to ease into it to make the transition from our former company seamless. We did not want to put ourselves in jeopardy of being sued for cross recruiting, which is heavily frowned upon in network marketing. We operate from a place of high integrity because that's the only way to do things. Integrity is something you cannot put a price tag on.

After the dust settled from the massive disruption that was taking place in our previous company and within our team, we decided to go full throttle with our new venture. I went to the doctor in March of 2013 for a routine checkup and he couldn't believe how great I looked. By this time, I had already started going back to the gym and working out. I mostly did cardio and leg workouts. I didn't touch weights at all. I didn't want to rupture my leads or tear the healing scar tissue. Besides, I was instructed not to lift anything more than ten pounds or lift anything above my head, so I didn't. But that didn't stop me from walking on the treadmill and doing light leg workouts. I was feeling great and I felt a significant increase in my energy level, too. After spending approximately two hours at the doctor's office, he gave me a clean bill of health. He said, "All of your blood work is normal. Your heart sounds good and you look great. Are you lifting weights?"

"No, sir," I said, "you advised me not to for at least six months, so I haven't touched them. I do walk on the treadmill four times a week for thirty mins at a time as well as light leg workouts, but no upper body at all."

"Wow, okay, that's awesome. How do you feel after you've finished that exercise regimen?"

"I feel great! No shortness of breath or extreme fatigue."

"I'm so impressed with how you look with all that you have been through," he said. "You were dead. Do you realize that?"

"Yes, I do, but I still can't connect to it because I don't remember anything about it. I see the pictures of me connected to all those tubes and wires like the six-million-dollar man but I can't believe it. It's almost as if it never happened to me. Rachel's experience was much different from mine, obviously. She can't even look at the pictures without crying. She doesn't like to talk about it much, either. I don't feel that way. I believe it's a blessing that I don't remember, because if I did, I might probably lose my mind."

"I agree with you," he said. "Well, you look great and I'm glad to see that you're still with us. What happened with you doesn't typically happen. By the way, I'm taking you off of your six-month restriction. You can go back to resuming your normal life. That includes driving your car."

"Doc, are you serious? I can go back to driving my car? Rachel doesn't have to chauffer me around anymore? Thank you so much!" The operative word I heard him say to me was "normal" because that's all I ever wanted to be. I didn't want to be treated differently or looked upon as a handicapped person. Once he said that to me, it validated everything I had been feeling about getting back to the routine flow of things.

I left his office and stood in the courtyard area for a few minutes just enjoying the sunny sky and the warm breeze on my face. I began to shed a tear as I was all of sudden overrun with emotion. A little old lady was walking toward the building and she stopped when she saw me. She said, "Young man, why are you crying?" I told her everything that I had been through and that the doctor cleared me to go back to my normal life. She also began to cry and she asked if she could pray for me. I told her certainly, by all means. I needed all the prayer I could get.

The woman prayed for me in front of the building and I floated back to my car and drove home. I called everyone and told them what the doctor had said to me and it was that day that the fire was lit under me to really get things moving into high gear with my life. I asked the empowering question of how could I improve my health and I received my answer. I took action and started using this nutrition program that helped put me on the right track. The doctor just confirmed it.

The business of helping to free people from physical and financial pain made more and more sense every day. I felt so great and so confident about my life and my future that I wanted everyone to feel the exact same way about theirs. I knew there was no way I couldn't get involved in this business and share this gift of awesome nutrition with the world.

Later that day, I was sitting in my home office, making a list of everyone that I knew that wanted to get healthy and live a more prosperous lifestyle. Rachel and I spoke about who we were going to share this with. We were so excited because we were back at phase one.

This is what we had been teaching our team to do for years and it had now come back full circle. Only this time, we were going to do it bigger and better all over the world.

We hit the ground running and began sharing the good news of this company with everyone that came in our path and our team exploded. We connected with people from Australia, New Zealand, Mexico, Colombia, I mean, it was just phenomenal. We had never experienced anything like this in our careers ever before. After a short while of building in our new company, we knew that we had found a home where we could plant our flag and create something incredibly special for as long as God saw fit for us to be there.

We caught the vision and saw how we were instrumental in helping to change the lives of so many people. It was a little overwhelming at first to have grown men thanking me and crying tears of joy over the phone and in person because their health had been returned to them. By implementing the nutrition plan into their daily lives and making it a lifestyle change, they were able to reclaim their health and reconnect with who they were as men. Some became better fathers, sons, husbands and the same happened with the women. We had become agents of change and were a symbol of hope and inspiration for everyone in the company around the world.

We were honored to receive the prestigious Heart of Isagenix Award in January 2015. This award is given to worthy candidates that represent the company's mission of helping to free people from physical and financial pain as well as inspiring others to become better. I remember being on stage with Rachel along with the founders of the company looking at an audience of over 5000 people in Palm Springs, California, thinking to myself, how wonderful God is.

I couldn't envision this day at all, yet there I stood on that stage and all I could hear were cheers and applause. I felt like a rock star. Rachel spoke with so much elegance and joy because we had both come a long way since the cardiac arrest. As she started crying, I looked at her and the only thing I could do was smile. I was frozen on the inside with pure joy and I was overflowing with gratitude. My Tsunami was over. The water had receded back into the ocean and everything was falling into place. We had to go through one of the most tragic situations in order to put us on track to really fulfill our destiny. I just didn't see it that way at the time, though. It's funny how that works. You never know how things are going to happen to put you where you need to be. The mess that you go through in life will eventually become your message. It's your pain and you overcoming that pain that builds your character. What doesn't destroy you only makes you stronger and I felt all of that. My life flashed in front of me in a split second and I was able to see into the future as to what my role was going to be going forward. Silently, I claimed victory in that moment on stage. I now understood why my life was spared and what the next steps were going to be.

There's a saying that the two most important days of your life are the day you were born and the day you discover why. Standing on stage that day told me exactly why.

CHAPTER 13

YOU MUST HAVE A CLEAR VISION FOR YOUR LIFE

Vision, what is that? Vision is simply your plan for your life. It sounds a lot simpler than it really is. Most people do not have a clear vision for their lives. They have no clue what their purpose is, so they are blowing in the wind like tumbleweeds doing everything except the one thing they were born to do.

If you were to ask ten people who they were, they more than likely would answer you by telling you their name and describing their occupation. For many people, their job or business defines them. The truth of the matter is that everyone has a clear and distinct purpose for being alive. The challenge is discovering what that purpose is. Some people discover it early in life, some people, later on, and others never discover it all. I believe one of the biggest tragedies in life is living and not knowing exactly why you were born. It almost seems a terrible waste of time. Rachel and I shared in this incredible experience and I certainly would not be alive today had it not been for her being there. But what did this all mean for us?

We meditated on it and our vision became clearer and clearer. Dr. Munroe talked about discovering your purpose in the

143

following manner. He said that the fact that you are alive is an indication that there is something that this world still needs from you. Whatever it is that makes you angry more than likely is the problem you were born to solve. When I thought about that statement, it really provided me with even more clarity.

The next step I took was to write out my life plan just like I had written down my goals. I had to design the outcome that I wanted to see happen in my life over the next several years. I gain the most joy when I'm in the midst of helping people overcome whatever obstacles hold them back from achieving what they truly desire. I love the feeling of extreme gratitude when people come up to me to thank me for inspiring them or helping them in some way. To know that my existence in this world made another person's life better whether in a small or big way makes feel so awesome. Especially now since I've gone through my own personal struggles with my health, business, etc. I felt that I could really help make a difference in other peoples' lives by offering them the best nutrition in the world and to coach them in pressing through the mental aspect of their challenges.

I believe my mental toughness is one of my strengths that I inherited from my mother. I developed that toughness by leaning on God and He continues to give me the strength to keep moving forward. I delight in sharing that strength with others who may not be as strong and need some direction. God uses us to answer all of our prayers whatever they may be. I consider myself an answer to my tribe's prayers. There are people praying for the things that I have in me—information, strength, courage, clarity—and my job is to show up in their lives at the right time to give it to them. I'm crystal clear on that and this clarity is the source of my discipline that I exercise daily in my life.

When you have a clear vision for your life, life tends to get easier. It simplifies it. It defines what you do and it shows you your destiny. Your destiny dictates your decisions, which ultimately dictate your results. Everything that you do should be motivated by your vision. It helps you identify yourself. Once I understood what my purpose for my life was, it explained why I had that unsettling feeling in the pit of my stomach for all of those years. I was helping people by providing them with a legal aid service but it was only a way for me to generate money. It was not my passion. It did not make me want to jump out of bed with enthusiasm. I didn't feel like I was making an impact in someone's life by helping them become a better human being. Better human beings make the world a better place to live. It's part of the cycle of life and the rhythm of the universe. Everything and everyone needs each other because we are all connected. I was longing to get back to a feeling of being connected but I just couldn't identify what the feeling was. It was sticking me in my side the whole time but I just ignored it and kept selling my legal plans. I continued to train the team and go with the flow because I had programmed my mind to do so. But deep in my heart, there was something else brewing and, unfortunately, it would have been ignored forever had I not died and come back to life.

I believe once again someone or something was trying to get my attention on a metaphysical and spiritual level. The reason I say this is because the night of my cardiac arrest, everyone was in place. Rachel was in the bed with me not in the bathroom. She called 9-1-1 and they talked her through what to do as far as administering CPR and she did it perfectly. She did not panic or run out of the house like most people may have done. She kept her wits about her and focused on the task at hand, which was saving my life. The four firemen from Station 38 arrived on the scene and took over from where she left off. They each did 300 chest compressions on me and shocked me six times with the defibrillator. The medics arrived and took over from where the firemen left off and they conducted another procedure on me, which froze my body to hypothermic levels. It blows me away to even think about what happened.

When I later spoke with Captain Cuff about why he didn't stop shocking me with the defibrillator after the first three or four attempts, he simply said there was no way they were going to lose me. He later went on to tell me how everything happened like clockwork. My cardiac arrest was a textbook save. He said he couldn't have created a more perfect scenario of people on the scene and everyone doing their part to help save my life. It was truly meant to be. In any other situation, another person would have certainly died.

When I look back on everything, I can say with the utmost confidence that it was a divine orchestrated plan that saved my life. I know I'm not the only one who has gone through something like this, but I'm the only one I know that has an attitude of gratitude like mine. I've met many survivors since then and a lot of them sound ungrateful to be alive. My mind has evolved so far beyond focusing on negativity that I almost can't see it. I'm aware that it's all around me in every form you can imagine but I just don't focus on it because it's not a part of my vision for my life. If it doesn't serve me, I don't do it.

I've learned over the years to always ask empowering questions to get the empowering answer. How does this serve me? What outcome am I looking to achieve? Is this going to bring me closer to it or push me further away? If it's not going to bring me closer to it, I simply don't acknowledge it. A man with a clear vision for his life lives a very narrow life, meaning he knows exactly what to do and what not to do. Your vision chooses everything in your life. It chooses what you read, how you spend your time, who you spend it with, how you spend your money, your to-do list, and your friends. It chooses your diet and your priorities.

A man without a vision lives a very loose life. Have you ever heard of the phrase "jack of all trades" and the "master of none"? That's the description of a man without a clear vision for his life. He's just all over the place, wasting time, blowing money, and at the end of the day, has nothing to show for it. He's easily distracted by foolishness and has no idea of what his true identity is.

His life is completely unfulfilled and he feels lost every day. He may wear a smile on his face by day, but behind closed doors he's miserable. You can only find true happiness in your life when you discover what your true purpose is. Your vision is internal not external, so don't look for a person or thing to bring it to you. God hid everything that a thing is supposed to become in itself. The challenge is digging deep enough inside your soul to discover what that is.

In just a few short years, Rachel and I have created an incredible global enterprise and we are rising leaders in this new venture. We are so blessed to have been positioned for absolute greatness within this organization. We connect with hundreds, even thousands of people daily through social media and other platforms that hear our voices, and we continue to make a positive impact on their lives. We are on a mission to become the best leaders of likeminded men and women all over the globe. We need more free thinkers, more doers, more love because the world is spiraling into a really dark place. There are so many people that are hurting and looking for a way out of their personal misery and we want to be the shining light showing them the way to freedom.

I've been given a third chance at life and I made a promise to God that I will not waste my time this go 'round. I will not waste a second on things that do not coincide with my vision for life. My vision is the vision that God has for me. It's my date with destiny and I will not stand her up. All things moving forward in my life have got to be taking me closer and closer to my final destination of purpose. To sum it all up, *if it doesn't evolve me, it will not involve me.* I have this written all over my house. It is my personal mantra and I share this concept with everyone that I meet. Adopting this philosophy will certainly keep you on track and help you eliminate the distractions in your life. Your greatest enemy to achieving success is not lack of intelligence or knowledge, but distraction. You can have all of the intelligence, knowledge, and desire in the world, but if you are constantly being distracted by things that come up, you will not achieve anything at all.

We are all here on this planet for a short time. What are you going to do with the time that you have? After dying and coming back to life and really doing a lot of soul searching, I realized that I learned a lot of valuable lessons but I also wasted precious time. I believe that God gave me a third chance to get it right. The mere thought of this just blows me away. There are many people that are not as fortunate, though. I don't know why some people live and are blessed with a second or third chance and many more are not. I don't try to figure that out because that's beyond my realm of understanding. However, I do know that if you're given a second or third chance to get things right, you shouldn't waste time doing things that are not taking you anywhere near your desired destiny.

So, let's recap. Your vision is your plan for your life. It should be so crystal clear that you can see yourself living in it every day. True happiness comes not from an external force but from a place deep inside of you. Everything that you do should be done with the intention of taking you closer to that vision. If not, you might be wasting valuable time. And time is the most precious commodity that there is. It's the only thing you cannot manufacture or buy more of. Once it's invested, it's gone forever. So, doesn't it make sense to invest it wisely?

As I reflect on the days I was lying in that hospital bed after suffering sudden cardiac arrest, the last thing I thought about was how much money I had or needed to make. I could care less about creating millions of dollars. I didn't think about the houses I had or my car or any material possessions. The thing I thought about most was how I could get more time. I was only forty years old and I had come to the resolve that I really hadn't done anything significant with my life. I didn't have any children to leave my legacy to.

Rachel and I were just starting our lives together and there was still so much for us to do. I didn't want to miss out on that. However, I needed more time to do it.

I thought about all of things I had done in the past that was such a waste of time and energy. It all came flooding through my mind like that Tsunami I mentioned earlier. So, when it comes to really being focused and getting in tune with your purpose or vision for your life, it's the most important thing you can do. Everything that is created has a purpose and was specifically designed to fulfill it. The manufacturer of your TV, car, phone, knows exactly what it is and how it was designed to operate. It comes with directions or a manual that explains what each feature is so you don't misuse it. Once you understand how to use it, you won't abuse it. If you don't understand the purpose of a thing, you can easily misuse it. I know many people that take better care of their cars than they do their own bodies because they know the purpose of the car. The car takes them to and from work every day. It allows them to take their kids to school and pick them up. It also allows them to pick up groceries from the supermarket. In other words, it meets their basic needs, and when the needs are met, all is right with the world. The car requires gasoline and regularly scheduled maintenance in order to last so it can continue meeting those needs.

A person, on the other hand, that does not know what his or her purpose is, tends to abuse themselves. You can plainly see it. For example, we have a major problem with obesity and disease in the United States. Many people do not feed the body what it needs in the way of good nutrition even with evidence that the foods they are consuming are causing them bodily harm. Instead, they feed it pleasure foods that cause obesity, diabetes, etc. They don't exercise regularly. They feed their minds garbage via trashy books, magazines, movies, etc. They disconnect themselves from the manufacturer and either don't have a copy of the manual or simply don't refer to it. Without the manual, it's impossible to develop a clear vision, and without the vision, nothing happens. They live an empty, unfulfilled life. When you understand that life is all about having a crystal-clear vision, everything you do should be taking you toward that, it really is just that simple. We overcomplicate it with everything else that doesn't matter and our minds are literally clouded with junk thoughts. Many people need a checkup from the neck up because they suffer from a severe case of "stinking thinking".

There is nothing worse than wasted potential. Have you ever met someone that had so much talent and could have become a mega superstar in that particular area of life but somehow managed to sabotage themselves and throw it all away? Was that person you? My life has been spared to help guide those individuals that have the potential to become absolutely outstanding but need a little guidance to get there. To know that I have the power and the opportunity to positively impact someone's life is why I breathe today.

Today, I am FIRED UP! I live each day knowing, believing, and stating to myself that if it doesn't evolve me, it will not involve me. I am still here and I am a champion! I've been given yet another chance and I'm not going to blow it. For the first time in ten years my heart is now functioning normally! I get teary-eyed just thinking about it because I know how far I've come. It's been one heck of a journey but one I wouldn't trade for the world.

Sure, I would have loved to skip all of the health challenges and the financial ups and downs, but if I had I wouldn't be the champion that I am today. I wouldn't be able to look someone else in the eye and tell them, it's going to be okay and you can do this, too. You can get healthy and create millions of dollars in the world of networking and marketing. You can be the author of a bestselling book. You can rise from the ashes like a phoenix and start anew with a renewed vision and a crystal-clear focus. You can change the world if you're not afraid to own your power and boldly run toward your destiny. Don't stand her up. Destiny doesn't like that. She wants to hug you and squeeze you and shower you with more love than you can stand. She wants to see you riding high and achieve your full beauty, meaning your fullest potential. She wants you to celebrate and be remembered for impacting the lives of your tribe. The very fact that you are alive today means that you have yet to fulfill your date with destiny.

Are you running as fast as you can toward her?

Be diligent in your pursuit and never take your eyes off your vision. You are more than a conqueror! I'm walking boldly in my power and I have no fear. Remember you are given a specific amount of time to fulfill your destiny in life. Don't waste a second doing anything that does not take you closer to achieving your vision. Time is of the essence!

When it comes to dealing with adversity, no matter how big or small that situation may be, I want you to consider this. Have you ever heard the story of King David and Goliath? Goliath was a Philistine giant that measured over nine feet tall, wearing full armor and he came out each day for forty days challenging the Israelites to fight. King Saul was the leader of the Israelites but he refused to fight the giant when he saw him. A little shepherd boy by the name of David said, "I'll fight him."

When he stepped up to the challenge, the Philistines laughed at him because he was just a little shepherd boy facing this huge giant, the biggest, strongest, and toughest warrior the Philistines had in their army. They all believed this boy would be eaten alive, the Israelites most certainly becoming their slaves. But David stood his ground and he didn't give in to the giant. He said these words which we know as a Psalm of David. "Yea, though I walk through the valley of the shadow of death, I will fear no evil: for thou art with me; thy rod and thy staff they comfort me." He then put the rock in his slingshot and hit Goliath in his head with it. The giant fell down and the battle was over just as quickly as it started. David was praised by his people and he later became King David, his name now forever synonymous with defeating the giant.

What if he hadn't stepped up to the challenge and answered the call? What if he stood in the shadows like all of the other Israelites, looking around to see if someone else was going to do it? At that particular moment in time, his destiny called him and he answered. He had the courage to step up to the challenge and defeat it. He didn't attempt to wish it away or pray it away, he had to slay it in order to defeat it and get past it. Without Goliath, we would never know who David was and no one would be talking about him today. It was the overcoming of a major obstacle in his life that brought him to his destiny. Many times, when people are faced with a Goliath in their life, they try to wish it away or pray it away but don't realize that the very thing they are trying to pray away is the very thing that will elevate them to a higher level in their lives. It's an opportunity to exercise their courage and faith to defeat whatever that Goliath represents in their life and show the world what they are made of. Whether it's a major health challenge, bankrupt business, divorce, loss of a loved one, lost employment, it doesn't matter. Sometimes these things that appear to be giants in our lives are the very things we must slay in order to reach greatness. Everyone at some point in time will face their Goliath. The question is, what will you do when it's your time?

Your belief in yourself is your highest form of influencing yourself to do whatever you desire to accomplish. When you truly understand this idea, an entirely new world will appear before your very eyes. You will be exposed to a new level of awareness and you will see life from a totally different perspective. You will also begin to understand that life is all about peeling back layers of awareness off the proverbial onion until you finally get to the core truth. That truth is discovering who you really are which is a spirit of infinite possibility, capable of creating anything and everything that can be imagined. It takes just as much energy to imagine big things as it does small things.

Whatever you are doing with your life at this very moment, I pray that you are doing it big! Playing small is a terrible waste of your potential and it serves no one. You were born with the Heart of a Champion! All of what you need to reach your highest self, you possess inside you. Thought plus conviction equals manifestation.

68776609R00089

Made in the USA
Columbia, SC
11 August 2019